COSMIC TELEPATHY
A HOW-TO STUDY GUIDE
TO MENTAL TELEPATHY

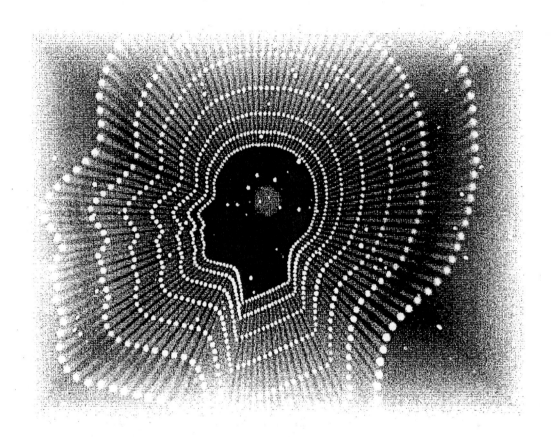

By Tuella
And
T. Lobsang Rampa

INNER LIGHT PUBLICATIONS

COSMIC TELEPATHY

ISBN: 1892062623

Timothy Green Beckley, Publisher
Carol Ann Rodriguez, Editorial Consultant
Tim Swartz, Cover Graphics & New Text

For a free weekly news letter on the web only at
www.ConspiracyJournal.com

For permission to reprint specific portions or to inquire about
foreign rights, address requests to Inner Light Rights Department
Box 753, New Brunswick, NJ 08903   MRUFO@webtv.net

Cosmic Telepathy

Understanding the Language of the Universe
By T. Lobsang Rampa

A sheet of cold whiteness completely enveloped my senses. For me, the world had utterly disappeared in an icy blast of wind and fury that seemed to swirl reality away like sand off a sidewalk. I knew instantly that I was in real danger and an awful sick feeling welled up inside me as I realized that there was nothing I could do about it.

I was helpless.

Less than an hour had passed since I had been happily trudging on a path that was to take me to a small monastery where I was to be allowed to look at some ancient and rare books. Having been born in Tibet I was well aware of the dangers of hiking alone in the mountains. But the terrain was familiar and the weather beautiful when I set out on what was supposed to be an hour's walk to keep my appointment. But the Himalayas, like the gods of old, can change their mood in an instant. Turning from gentle lover to shrieking harpy in the blink of an eye.

My first hint of trouble was when the wind shifted around and began to blow straight into my face. A gray blanket of clouds soon settled down over the land, but instead of offering warm comfort, this quilt brought stinging snowflakes whipped into a blinding frenzy. The storm completely disorientated me, as I stood exposed to the storm unable to move for fear of wandering off the path and plunging into the numerous rocky gorges that surrounded me. I was completely alone.

My mind raced as I frantically tried to think of a way out of my predicament. More experienced men than me had died under similar circumstances, but I was determined not to become another statistic of the mountains.

I thought about the monastery that I had been heading to. The monks would be expecting me and with the unexpected change in the weather, would be worried about my safety. That, I figured, could be something that I could work with.

Even though the wind screamed like a banshee in my ears, I mustered all of my internal strength and set about quieting my mind. Never before had I attempted such a mental feat under such stressful conditions. But my life now depended on my ability to tap into that secret place in my inner being and throw off the shackles of the physical.

Soon the outside world with its unpleasantness faded into the distance. I could have been floating in the emptiness of space so removed from the environment was I. My mind was no longer confined to the small vessel that was my body. It was now free to explode outwards in an energetic burst of power that hopefully would carry it to the monastery and seek out a kindred spirit within.

My thoughts were like a laser beam with one goal in mind, to communicate my distress to someone within range to help. With my inner eye I could see the monastery and the bright glow around it coming from all of the enlightened souls that dwelt within it. This glow, made up from the individual auras of the monks, acted as a homing beacon to my concentrated thoughts. One aura in particular drew my consciousness to it like a moth to a flame.

An unfamiliar face swam into view. It was the face of a young monk who was turning clockwise a series of traditional Tibetan prayer wheels (Mani wheels) located in a dark corridor of the monastery. His aura was a glorious bright gold in color that radiated a magnetic energy that drew me in. When my consciousness reached the monks aura he immediately stopped and without hesitation, hustled off down the corridor to seek help. At the same time he sent powerful, comforting thoughts of warmth and friendship, assuring me that I would soon be rescued. With that, I withdrew my thoughts from his mind and shook myself to full consciousness.

I squatted close to the ground and huddled against the raging storm, knowing that help was on the way. It wasn't long before a search party from the monastery came down the pass to escort me the rest of the way.

Inside the monastery as I sat and warmed myself with cups of hot, sweet tea, I got to meet and thank the young monk who picked up on my thoughts and sent for help. We talked for several hours on the mysteries of the universe and the powers of the human spirit. We became good friends, kindred spirits you might say, and whenever I travel to Tibet, I always make my way to that small, isolated monastery to see my friend. It no longer surprises me to find that he knows of my imminent arrival days before I actually appear.

Ah, the mysteries of the universe.

WE ARE ALL CONNECTED

The word telepathy is derived from the two separate Greek words Tele meaning "far off" or "from a distance," and Pathy which means, "to feel." Simply looking at the origin and meanings of this word already gives us a clear idea of the definition. However, the dictionary goes one step further and defines telepathy as "apparent communication from one mind to another..."

Telepathy is the ability to be aware of thoughts and send and receive them. Telepathy is fairly common to some degree. The most common type is between close family or friends and manifests as answering questions before they are asked, knowing when a family member is thinking of you, or thinking about them and they call. The other is telepathic communication with large groups of people at the same time. Many great teachers throughout the ages used this form of telepathy in teaching their students.

Slightly less common is the ability to read the surface thoughts of strangers. Even less common is being able to read the deep or subconscious thoughts of people, friends, family or anyone else. It is not, however, completely unknown. If you have the disconcerting habit of knowing everything about a person when you meet them, you are at least a highly gifted telepath. Nevertheless, all human beings have the ability to communicate by the process that has come to be known as telepathy.

Why develop your telepathy when we have virtually instant global communication available through technology? The main reason is that psychic thought pollution constantly surrounds us. Millions of minds on the planet are radiating their thoughts 24 hours a day – much like a radio station. But instead of broadcasting top 40 hits, these minds are broadcasting their innermost thoughts and feelings. This is why you often can't think straight when you are tired. You are picking up psychic thought pollution. Most of the time the natural filters in our heads tune these "outside" thoughts out. Without filters, we would be bombarded into salivating idiots unable to recognize our own thoughts from the thoughts of everyone else.

Cosmic Telepathy

However, even with our natural filters, stray, outside thoughts do manage to work their way into our minds without our conscious knowledge or permission. These thoughts can have dire influence on the way we handle stressful situations, or even how we deal with our usual, daily lives.

We have all heard in the news about individuals who, completely out of character, have suddenly committed the most horrific crimes. Often this is the result of someone who has been under the influence of outside thoughts. Developing telepathy will not only strengthen your natural mental filters from outside influence, it can also develop your other psychic abilities to a highly advanced state.

So, do you want to have a clear head? Think clearly? Have more certainty in making the correct decision for yourself? Then, learning how to be aware of your telepathic ability is a must. You don't have to use it to communicate with other people, but you will. What's important first is to be able to have your own thoughts for a change.

THOUGHT POLLUTION

In crowds, thought pollution may manifest as "white noise" or constant buzzing in the ears (brain), accompanied by a feeling of pressure on the brain. This is due to the constant noise of all of the thoughts of others that one is unable to block.

Many highly gifted telepaths are unable to live in highly populated areas, and an apartment complex is a nightmare. They are also prone to intense headaches. This gift may or may not be related to proximity. For strangers, it is usual that the person must be close by (though not always the case). Family members seem to be instantly accessible, due to the non-local nature of the gift, speed of light laws do not apply.

Strong thought, as in a disaster or violent attack, may be picked up without prior knowledge of the person at all, if they are in the vicinity or there are enough people concentrating on mentally screaming at the top of their lungs. Telepathy also manifests more strongly if one really desires something (a strong focus of will or emotion).

How can you tell the difference between your thoughts and intruding thoughts from outside of your own mind? If it's not yours, you can't control it. If you are picking up someone else's thought, it keeps coming back until they stop thinking it or you change the channel you're listening to. You can't change the thought itself because you're just listening in.

You can also tell because you won't want the thought in most cases. Your true thoughts come from within your own soul. These thoughts are creative and help you grow. They benefit you spiritually. Other people's thoughts can contain pain. When you pick up that thought and you don't know that it's not yours, you can start to produce the pain in yourself. Then, you go try to treat the pain. And on and on you go creating a whole scenario off of someone else's thoughts.

Telepathy can manifest in three ways. A sending telepath cannot "hear" the thoughts of others, but instead broadcasts his/her own thoughts to anyone even remotely sensitive. A sending telepath can influence others, without being aware of it, by strongly desiring something. A danger is that one who is a sending telepath, without any of the other gifts, has a tendency to be self-centered and demanding, and petulant when they don't get their way.

Cosmic Telepathy

A receiving telepath can "hear" but can't send. This person might believe the voices, thoughts, or impressions of ideas to be internally generated, and might doubt their sanity. As is often the case, the thoughts are incongruous, and seem to come from nowhere, but the individual cannot distinguish the internal thought from the external.

Most common is one who can both send and receive, and the response is usually enough to convince the person that they are not crazy, though the gift might be hidden out of a fear of being unusual. The "voices" or impressions gathered by the telepath are relaying accurate, verifiable information based on the consensual hallucination we call reality. The information is usually pretty mundane, and the telepath, upon thinking about it, can learn to tell their thoughts from those that leaked in from the outside.

Telepathy, like all psychic abilities, is the natural capabilities of the soul. Everyone is psychic. Contrary to popular misconception, psychic ability isn't limited to predicting the future or being able to read what someone is thinking. It takes psychic ability even to breathe. All your so-called "normal" abilities are psychic abilities. What many people term "psychic" is merely a deeper, more profound level of those normal abilities such as seeing, hearing, feeling, tasting, smelling, knowing, moving and creating.

It's not that one person is totally psychic and another isn't psychic at all. Psychic awareness and abilities are sacred gifts given to each of us. The difference is only in how much each of us chooses to develop them. The choice is not an intellectual one, but a spiritual one. We naturally develop those abilities associated with our interests just as those who are interested in music, art or computers develop abilities that help them become more capable in those endeavors. We pursue our interests more passionately and seek out more understanding, instruction and practice.

The same applies to psychic development and spiritual growth. Perhaps the most important aspect of psychic development is to deepen and expand your awareness of your true spiritual self. Telepathy and all psychic abilities are different expressions of the same oneness of being.

The main reason our telepathic powers are not more commonly used is because we are not taught how to use it. There has been many accounts describing the occurrence of telepathy throughout history, and it was originally described as the power of the "third eye" – which humanity later altered to describe seeing elements in the spiritual world. Modern studies and tests have verified that telepathy exists not only in the human, but also in the animal, and plant kingdoms.

As far back as 4,000 BC in Egypt and Mesopotamia there have been descriptions of telepathy. Many of the legitimate historical accounts sound like cases you hear about today. One case, a hysterical Greek woman around 340 BC, claims she "saw" the death of her brother in a "daydream." Months later, the skeptical villagers found out her brother did indeed die on that day – in a far-off battle. Little has changed since that time. The faces may change, but telepathy remains constant throughout time and space.

Telepathy seems to occur in distinct patterns, depending on whether the sender and receiver are within sight of each other. One pattern of telepathy involves distance, where the subjects are not within sight of each other and usually a picture, impression, or feeling is received by one party. The distance does not seem to be a factor. Telepathy has occurred from those who were several streets apart, to those who were half way around the world.

Cosmic Telepathy

BEYOND THE PHYSICAL UNIVERSE

Telepathy appears to transfer thoughts beyond the physical and on the spiritual plane, for the feelings one had while picking up the thoughts were often described as being similar to a "spiritual experience." Since the communication appears to travel instantaneously, we can assume that our thoughts are somehow traveling outside the physical universe, as we know it.

Besides the image of the circumstance being "seen," many of the "messages" received also gave one strong impressions, or feelings. Quite often these were described as an "enlightening experience," or of having a "dream" while being awake. This would indicate the spiritual body could use the same processes to deliver telepathic experience as it does to communicate the dreams we have at night.

Much of our understanding of the invisible universe depends on knowledge and handling of invisible energies. To handle energies that are not visible seems to be one of the main characteristics of human beings.

This characteristic is the result of the human capability to abstract. It is the probing into what is beyond the scope of everyday experience that eventually led mankind to modern technologies, and to modern concepts of space and time. Knowledge of the laws governing electromagnetic energies determines practically all contemporary theory of the universe, from descriptions of majestic galaxies all the way down to sub-atomic physics.

Visible night is but a small section of the large electromagnetic vibrations. Most of this spectrum is invisible to the human eye. Analysis of the concepts of visible light and the expansion these concepts led to knowledge of the electromagnetic energy and its many applications in modern technologies. We can explain many of the phenomena of heat, acoustics, chemical reactions, etc., as being part of the same expressions of electromagnetic energy.

There is another energy that mankind has experienced from the beginning. This energy that mankind seems even more mysterious because of its seeming elusiveness. We cannot see it as easily as we can see visible light, nor can we feel it as markedly as heat. This energy is life force. It is everywhere around us. In other words, we are in an ocean of energy of both life forces and of electromagnetic waves.

Life force has received many names throughout the ages:

- People of ancient India called it PRANA. The practices of pranayama and yoga evolved from knowledge of prana.

- The ancient Chinese called it CHI. The practices of Tai and Chi Gong came from this knowledge.

- The Polynesians called the mysterious life force mana, and derived from it the practices of kahuna.

- Practitioners in the West used many words for this energy: life force, animal magnetism, solar ether, odic force, psychic, and many more.

Cosmic Telepathy

Serious scientist of all ages knew of this energy, and recently they formulated some very basic characteristics of this psychic energy, or life force. These scientists found out that there are considerable differences between life energy and electromagnetic energy. In some way, both energies act like opposite polarities of one and the same basic principle. Of both forms of energy, only a small fraction is perceivable by human beings with the apparatus of their senses. Both energies pulsate. That's what these energies have in common.

The difference between the two energy forms is very important.

Energies that belong to the electromagnetic spectrum of light tend to achieve a balance when a higher potential gets in contact with a cold one, a lower potential. If you bring a hot body in contact with a cold one, a heat exchange occurs until both bodies have the same temperature. Physicists call this process this process entropy.

With life force, the opposite is the case. When a body of high life force potential comes in contact with a body of lower potential, a process takes place that we call negative entropy.

In this process the stronger potential draws energy from the weaker one, and it becomes stronger. Still more marked is the difference of the space in which both energies act. As we all know, the electromagnetic energies diminish in intensity with the square of the distance. That's why we need amplifiers of considerable strength if we want to pick up radio waves from a very distant radio transmitter. This principle is valid for the space-time continuum of the physicist.

People of all ages who used life energies knew of the power of telepathy. Once a person working with life energies such as a healer has a telepathic link, he or she can bridge time and space and establish a link to the target, no matter how distant the target may be. This ability takes time and patience. To become an adept at telepathy all modern notions of schedules or deadlines become insignificant. You will achieve your goal of telepathy when the time is right.

It is obvious that work with telepathy requires a new model of space. This model looks quite different from the space-time that the physicist describes. It is a hyper- space in which identical objects create direct contacts. Hyperspace is a theoretical term given to a reality outside the known physical universe. Enlightened, spiritual people throughout history have recognized these other planes of existence, so it comes to no surprise that science is now just starting to realize that there is more to our universe than what we can see with our physical senses.

Another aspect of telepathy is when both subjects can physically see each other, and communicate sensible, logical thoughts and instructions, without verbal words. Even though this is the rarest type of telepathy, oddly enough this type is the most common perception by the general public as to what telepathy is all about.

A magnetic energy field that pervades throughout the universe surrounds us all. These fields are similar to the kind that surrounds a magnet, except the energy fields that surround living things do not attract metals, but rather the electronic impulses from other living things. Thoughts and mental pictures are electronic impulses, be they in, or outside the brain. In the same way magnetic force "pull" metals and magnets together; life energy forces attract elements of many kinds between human beings. This happens between physical bodies, (sexual attraction, for example), mental bodies (between those who share the same beliefs or attitudes), and between spiritual bodies (for example, an attraction you may feel with one who you have shared a past life with).

Those who have surrounding energy fields of similar vibrations are the ones most likely to experience telepathy. This is why identical twins, and brother/sisters within five years of each other are ones with higher telepathic experiences. However, it is possible to have a telepathic communication with anyone who is also tuned in the same wavelength as yourself.

Most telepathic occurrences happened without either party consciously trying to communicate with the other. It was usually a tragic event one was going through, that the other "picked up" (by seeing or feeling the experience that the first party was going though). This indicates two attributes of telepathy: (1). It is not fully based on conscious thought, and (2). A strong focus of emotion is involved (resulting from a tragic or exciting event).

Since one need not be conscious of "sending" or "receiving" telepathic impulses, the subconscious or spiritual body (which is also electromagnetic in nature) plays a part in telepathy as well. For one to develop their telepathic powers, strong concentration, patience and meditation to link the spiritual, mental and emotional levels are needed.

One meditation to bring your spirit, mind, and emotions into harmony (or similar vibration) can be done so:

Find a quiet time and space where you can be undisturbed for about 20 minutes each day. Close your eyes, and with your imagination, try to "see" the energy field that surrounds you. After having an image appear, create different emotions (joy, fear, love, anger, etc.) and image these emotions flowing into the energy field you created around you. When completed, do the reverse (send the emotions which are flowing in the energy field back into your physical body.

Most of the time, an impulse will enter one's spiritual energy field (which acts as a giant "life force radar"), then travels to the emotions where the individual senses a "strange impression" – usually unexplainable. The mind does not have any explanation for this feeling, usually because the mind is not involved in the process – or does not believe in this process.

This meditation will help the mind become involved in this process, so that when you train later with a partner, you will be able to send and receive at will, rather than having the impression come by "accident."

PRACTICE MAKES PERFECT

To practice telepathy it is essential to believe in the entire concept of mind-to-mind communication. Skeptics reportedly have never scored high in psychic testing or experiments. A proper frame of mind is extremely important as a first step towards telepathy. You should have the positive attitude that what you are doing is real and worthwhile in order to get the creative juices flowing so to speak.

Telepathy works best when the other person you are mentally "linking" with is thinking about a subject that is interesting, colorful, exciting and/or emotional. This is because these types of thoughts are more energetic, and intense, therefore easier for you to pick up on.

Cosmic Telepathy

Try to keep all experiments and activities rather short to prevent boredom or fatigue from occurring. Your psychic ability is at its peak when you feel most energized.

Avoid trying too hard. Forcing yourself to sense what another person is thinking will actually sabotage your attempts. Your mind is primed for psychic perceptions when you are relaxed and at ease.

Being in positive health both mentally and physically makes telepathy easier. As mentioned before, being tired and sick makes accepting psychic perceptions much more difficult, as does feeling negative, depressed or generally sad. When under these conditions it is most common for mistakes or misperceptions to occur.

Be loose, relaxed and receptive. Achieving a mild state of meditation helps psychic perceptions "flow" easier. If the doors of your mind are closed, nothing can make its way in. Anything that you find distracting will be detrimental to your attempts. Try to always be in a calm and quiet environment to allow for maximum concentration.

Pay attention to the ways in which each and every psychic perception you have occurs. Closely monitor your different states of emotion during these sessions and examine whether they may or may not influence your perceptions. Telepathy is a skill rather than a talent, and like any skill developing it is a learning experience.

Don't be discouraged if you don't automatically understand your perceptions. Sometimes impressions can come to you in a symbolic or unusual, associative forms. Make an effort to analyze each of your impressions individually to the best of your abilities.

Each of the above points should help you develop your telepathic skills. One of the easiest experiments is to get with a friend who has a positive attitude towards your endeavor, separate yourself from them, and try to tune into their thoughts. Do this for a set period of time, recording your impressions, and then compare them with your partner. The more you do this (not necessarily with the same person) the more often you should get positive and accurate results.

CREATIVE VISUALIZATION – OPENING YOUR THIRD EYE

Right now take a few minutes to close your eyes and visualize something…an eagle soaring high over the mountains. Don't just think the words "eagle" and "mountains," but actually form a mental image of a majestic eagle high in the blue sky. Now hold this image in your mind for as long as possible.

Chances are it won't be long before other, stray thoughts start to intrude on your visualization. Problems at the office…the kids need to be taken to soccer practice…the cat just threw up on the rug. Your beautiful scene of blue skies and wildlife are now gone, replaced by the normal worries and problems that effect our everyday life.

This is why so many people find it impossible to continue developing their psychic powers and telepathy. It's not for a lack of desire, but more of a lack of learning to control and quiet your thoughts.

Everything we experience in "reality" has its beginnings in the non-physical. Every thought we think is a seed. Every time we think the same thought over again, we water that seed. When we think such a thought with emotion, we fertilize it. The more intense our desire or fear regarding such a thought, the more likely it is to come into our experience, and the faster it will manifest. Thoughts are just as real as actions, but exist at a much higher and faster frequency.

Our thoughts erupt from pure spirit or consciousness, like a spark. As we think it, it begins to slow, moving into the vibrational realm of feelings. We think the thought, and then we have a feeling about it. We might feel excited or nervous. Depending on our feelings about it, we then have more thoughts and more feelings, while deciding what to do. As this process unfolds, the vibrations slow, and we eventually move into the realm of action (or no action, if that is the decided course of action).

Julia Jablonski in her article: *Creative Visualization and the Law of Attraction*, writes that there is only one main law that must mastered in order to create what we want in our lives.

"It sounds simple, but it requires more conscious awareness of our thoughts than is ordinary. Of course, the more conscious and deliberate we are in choosing our thoughts, the more we are able to focus our experiences in desired directions. This is generally referred to as the Law of Attraction."

"Ask and ye shall receive" is a truth. We ask with our desire, with what we give our attention to. Our thoughts and feelings are magnetic, drawing that which is focused upon into our lives.

You may really want a particular job that would involve a promotion at work, for example. You may say to yourself (or the universe), "Oh, I would really love to have that job. I hope I get that job." While you're thinking this, you're also picturing yourself in that position, happy, fulfilled. You're imagining the new office, sitting at the new desk, performing the new tasks.

This is a powerful way to create what you are seeking. The universe responds to your desire impersonally, for it's not about whether or not you deserve it, it's about what you're in harmony with receiving. The All That Is of pure potentiality responds to the energy of you wanting that job, and being happy and fulfilled in that job.

By visualizing yourself in that job, you are already in the process of creating this in your experience. You only have to allow your thoughts and imaginings to filter down to manifest into the "reality" of this plane. And by controlling your thoughts, you can better realize your true needs and desires and send a clear message to the universe.

Some people naturally speak and think in ways that are effective; others have a habit of thinking in ineffective ways. One can often detect how deliberate a creator someone is by the way he or she expresses themselves. For example:

"I hope the weather stays nice like this. It's so beautiful out!" (This is effective for it leads to more beautiful weather) "I hope it doesn't rain! That would be terrible!" (This is ineffective, for it leads to rain and feelings that are not wanted.)

"I want to create harmony and happiness in this relationship. I know we can do it if we try." (This is effective, for it leads to harmony, happiness and empowerment.)

"I don't want to fight with you. I hate it when we fight. I can't take this anymore, this has to change!" (This is ineffective, leading to more fighting and frustration.)

"I've decided to move to San Francisco. There are lots and lots of people who have done this. There must be an infinite number of options for how I can make this happen. Let's see, I could..." (This is effective, leading to positive visualization and creative problem solving.)

Cosmic Telepathy

"I wish I could move to move to California, but I hear it's so expensive out there. The job market is tight, and a tiny apartment costs what a nice house costs here. And what about those earthquakes?" (Clearly, this is ineffective, unless one is trying to talk oneself out of it! This train of thought leads to negative, pessimistic feelings, and if the move is undertaken, undesirable experiences with finances and perhaps even earthquakes.)

In this last example, the effective person thinking or speaking has opened themselves not only to creative problem solving, but also to the limitless resources of the Universe. Their thoughts are "in line" with their desires. The ineffective thinker, however, sends energy in direct opposition to what is expressed as desired. Note also the difference in feeling between saying, "I wish..." which is weak and implies it's unlikely to happen, and "I've decided." Saying, "I've decided," sets things strongly into motion.

Following are some exercises or things to keep in mind as you begin to take more responsibility and control over what you attract into your life and to further your telepathic development.

- Pay attention to your fantasies. Daydreams (and night dreams) and the themes that run through our minds are like the trailers to movies. They show us what we're in the process of manifesting. If we're daydreaming about how we're afraid we're going to not make our sales quota, or how we may lose that important case in court, it's time to begin to shift gears and begin imagining ourselves creating what we do want. If we're daydreaming about choking our neighbor because her dog barks all night long, and because when we request help with the matter she's rude, it's wise to know that we're likely to experience more negativity from that neighbor, even if we're polite on the surface. Thoughts are things.

- Listen to yourself. Pay attention to your language. Especially watch yourself for phrases such as "I hope," "I wish," and "I've decided." Also, watch for "buts." The word "but" is used to contradict what was just expressed. Pay attention to how often you are talking about what you want, versus what you don't want. Let go of what you don't want, and shift to focusing on what you do.

- Try starting small. Imagine a small thing that you'd like to come to you. You're far less likely to have resistance to creating this in your experience, and your beliefs are likely to be less challenged by a smaller desire. As you get good at this, you can aim higher and higher, for your belief in your ability to create in your own experience will expand.

Try drawing a picture of what you're wanting in your life. Really allow yourself to get into the flow of picturing yourself in the future with everything as you want it to be. Or you might try writing a story about how you got from where you now are to where you want to be, as if it's already happened. The more you can suspend disbelief or resistance, the better.

Writing and drawing allow us to get out of what is "practical" and dream our way into what we want. Remember that the potential is unlimited. Your well-being does not come at the expense of others. Just as there is not a limited amount of "happiness" or "health" on the planet, there is no need to worry that you'll attract more than your share of anything. Your being happy does not mean someone else must be depressed to balance things out. In fact, you're being healthy, wealthy and wise makes it easier for others to follow in your footsteps.

It's important to appreciate those things in our experiences that we don't want, as well as the blessings we already have. Just as without darkness, we would not know light, so it is with contrast. When we experience something and we know we don't like it, we suddenly know what we do want. Thank the contrast, and pivot away from it with grace. Shoving away from it tends to ricochet us right back into it, for then we think of it with intense emotion. The more we can find peace with what we don't want, the easier it is to flow with intense desire toward what is wanted.

Also, it's good to embrace wanting. Desire is what keeps us alive. Without desire, we wouldn't be here. It's all about wanting to live, wanting to experience, wanting, wanting, wanting (not necessarily having, having, having). Perhaps we're very altruistic, and all we want to do is give, but this is still satisfying some desire in ourselves to give.

I'm not saying we should do whatever we want without regard to others. I'm saying that if we are in harmony with our inner being's desires, we will naturally want to do what is best for us, and this will naturally be what is also best for others. Sometimes, others may not see that at the time. We may want to end a relationship that another wants us to stay in. From a greater perspective, when we act in harmony with our own heart's desire to move toward something else, we afford that other person the opportunity to work through their own fears and dependencies.

THE IMPORTANCE OF PROPER MEDITATION

Meditation helps the physical conscious mind connect with the higher or divine consciousness we all have inside ourselves. Through practice and dedication, this "bridging" between our physical and divine selves opens the doors to a new spiritual knowledge that has always existed, but that we may not have been able to "tap" into.

People who meditate on a regular basis report feeling the "need" to improve their attitudes or outlooks on life. This could be one of the positive results of bridging the conscious and sub-conscious spiritual minds together. All of this is important for maintaining a positive energy flow for psychic development. The more positive your attitude is, the easier it is to make a connection to the positive forces around you.

There are numerous forms of meditation such as Yoga, Tai Chi, mantra, gazing and freeform; these are the most common. No one way is better than another. What works for one person may not work for another, so it's best for people to choose the type of meditation that feels the most comfortable for them. Then one must practice, practice, practice.

There are dozens of books on the market that describe how to meditate, or if you'd like, take a look at our method of meditation. The important part to any meditation though, is learning how set the energy within, how to protect yourself and align your energies with the higher forces on ethereal planes. Get a notebook and keep track of your experiences, your outlook and so on.

Cosmic Telepathy

First: Page 1: Define what spirituality is (from your perspective) and what it means to you. Tapping into psychic energies is above all else a spiritual experience.

Page 2: Define "why" you want to develop your psychic abilities.

Page 3: Write down the events, feelings etc., of your meditations during the week.

Doing these exercises should give you some insight into yourself as a spiritual being. A lot of people have "thought" about their spirituality, but I guarantee, when you start writing it down, you'll write things you never considered before. The "why" will help you identify the blocks that might stand in your way, so be honest with yourself in both these cases. That's the most important part; don't hold back, write what you truly feel. The last exercise gives you a picture of where you are now and makes a record for comparison later.

The process of developing one's telepathy is the process of becoming more "awake" in one's life. In sudden spiritual awakenings it can be like putting on glasses after years of not seeing with 20/20 vision, and not having known that one's vision was less than it could be. Usually, however, there is a more gradual development of psychic skills. Most humans can run, but a runner who practices and trains regularly, pushing himself to become better, faster, and more enduring, is clearly able to perform much better as a runner and with greater ease. Similarly, a psychic who has developed and improved upon his abilities is able to access information that is clearer and more accurate than can an untrained person, and is able to do this with much greater ease.

There are many positive aspects of becoming more aware through telepathy, but there are also some challenges that come with the territory. It can be disconcerting to be seeing things that no one else sees. One begins to feel fundamentally different from most people. It can be hard to "turn off" one's sensitivity, and being in crowds or around negative people can become very difficult. Sometimes the psychic may see into his/her own future, and it can become difficult to go with the flow in one's life when the outcome of a particular relationship or situation has been foreseen.

Telepathy also comes with a great deal of responsibility. Those who develop such ability must concurrently develop a greater sense of love and integrity, for not only will they have a greater affect on others; the repercussions of their own actions will be more dramatic and immediate. Spiritually, one is held to higher standards the more one develops. We are responsible for all the knowledge we possess.

Telepathy is a skill of the mind and imagination. Imagination does not mean it is not real. Psychics tend to be highly creative/imaginative types. Expand both your imagination and your ability to connect with the universe and "know" others with this exercise:

Begin by focusing on a rock, or other object of the mineral kingdom. Focus on this object for a few moments, then imagine your head expanding, opening, and becoming a part of that object. Your body is now "you," and your head is one with this object. How does it feel to be this object? Imagine it in great detail. What is it like inside of this object? Now continue and focus on a tree and then an animal. This exercise deepens one's ability to empathize and learn to become one with all.

Cosmic Telepathy

Introduction by Dragonstar

Author, How To Develop Your Latent Paranormal Powers

Tuella's "calling" as a Messenger of Light began in the early seventies with her channeling work commissioned personally by Ashtar on behalf of the Intergalactic Space Confederation. In addition to *Cosmic Telepathy: A How-To Study Guide to Mental Telepathy*, her books by Inner Light Publications include: *Messengers For the Coming Decade*, *Project World Evacuation*, and, *Ashtar—A Tribute*.

Tuella's channeled messages for this book reveal that every living thing has an aura, or energy field surrounding it. Though auras are constantly changing and moving, stored within them is everything about that person, from the moment they were born to the present day - all they have experienced, thought and felt. It's all ready to be tapped into...so long as you know the password. Equally as wonderful is the fact that an individual's energy can remain with everything it ever touches; it can even be captured in a photographic image. All this through the wonders of cosmic telepathy.

A few of the things that can lower your frequency and keep your cosmic telepathy from flowing properly: heavy, processed, and junk foods; try to eat lightly or not at all before any attempts at cosmic telepathy; negative words, thoughts, actions, and feelings; negative people and situations; artificial synthesized materials such as fluorescent lights, synthetic fabrics, synthetic foods, vitamins and medicines; working at a job you hate; mainstream radio, television, and newspapers – particularly the news.

We all have preconceived notions of how things should work out, how our dreams should manifest, what will happen when and how. We have beliefs that outline the only way things can happen, but when we have those outlines in our heads of the way it should happen, we slow it down, and sometimes stop it from happening at all.

It's not the circumstances that bring the reality to you. A good job doesn't ensure you'll be rich, secure and happy in that job. Your resonance determines whether you'll be rich, secure and happy. A good job can be the detail the universe chooses, but so could a great investment paying off that frees you to open your own business, or a neighbor deciding to live in Europe and asking you to run her business.

If you send out a pure energy of prosperity, security, ease, fun, etc. and let the universe decide how it arrives, you are opening every possible door that could bring you this reality. If you have rigid ideas of how and when and whether you can have what you want, you are closing the possible avenues of its arrival, one by one.

Know you can have everything you desire. Know that it will take time, patience, knowledge, skill and healing to open all the doors of possibility. The universe and your Higher Powers will take care of the details- if you do your part and become crystal clear about how you want it to feel when it arrives.

A PERSONAL PERSPECTIVE

Tuella wanted everyone to know that psychic abilities were available to anyone who had the desire and patience to learn how to use them. Tuella was consumed by a desire to research and develop techniques for communication via telepathy, and that her experiences and discoveries in this arena have fundamentally changed the way she related

Cosmic Telepathy

to others on a daily basis. Her channeled communications indicated that there were a number of easy exercises that were available to start the novice on the correct path towards cosmic telepathy.

This exercise requires a partner. Stand or sit facing each other. Have your partner close his/her eyes and hold out her hands with the palms up. Take your index finger and move it just above the palm of her hand, without touching the skin. Repeat this on both of your partner's hands, and as you are doing this, tighten you index finger up by contracting the muscles. Try to concentrate on the tip of your finger and imagine that it is drawing a shape on your partner's palm. The combination of the contracted muscles in your finger and your mental concentration will create a small electrical tingle on your partner's palms.

As you experiment, ask your partner which palm you are working on. If your partner cannot at first tell you, then tell her to open her eyes and look. With her eyes open, repeat the experiment, tracing over her palms as you did when her eyes were closed. Repeat this a few times, then have her close her eyes again and feel for the slight tingle of the cosmic telepathy signals. The first time you attempt this exercise, the results may be hard to see, but continue working with it and your results should improve.

If you don't see any improvement it may be because of a negative environment.

Being around negativity lowers the frequency. People who have worked on themselves and raised their frequency go out into the workplace, the mall, etc. and people of lower frequency suck their energy. The negativity of the thoughts and conversations those people are having and the electromagnetic radiation (EMF's) from TV and computer screens, fluorescent and halogen lights, is energetically draining. A person's energy can become so refined and sensitive that they literally can't handle being around "normal" people or crowds. It's exhausting, and it affects their health and energy level.

Anyone can go off to the mountains, the desert or an island and hang out only with people who have similar beliefs and frequencies, and thus live a life full of joy, love and grand spiritual/meditational experiences. The trick is to learn how to maintain your higher frequency and continue to live and function in the real world.

It's hard for many people to move past the draining effects of negativity. The great ones, however, learn to stay centered, pour forth love, and not become so drained they can't continue. A few methods commonly used to increase frequency include flower essences, therapeutic grade essential oils, meditation/prayer, time in nature, proper nutrition, hands-on healing techniques like Reiki and other energy therapies. As we increase our frequency we are changed: synchronicity speeds up, our thoughts create our reality more quickly, we become healthy, happy, and at peace with the world.

Let go of any unresolved energies or emotions that are binding you to the physical world. Whether it is unhealthy attachments to material pleasures or negative emotions – you need to release your resentments, your fears, your need to feed your ego. Forgive those who you feel have wronged you and judge nothing as less than divine, perfect in its own unique way.

Cosmic telepathy can open up other amazing avenues of psychic abilities within you. You will experience a whole new world of incredible perceptions and knowledge and see reality in ways that you never thought possible. Your journey begins with one step and the desire to be the enlightened being our creator intends us all to be.

Preface

Following the release of *Project World Evacuation* by the Intergalactic Council, I personally thought that my work with books was completed. It seemed to me that after its presentation, there was nothing left to say!

Nevertheless, within three months time, our Guardians announced that a book on Cosmic Telepathy would be needed and, at that time, released its title. They expressly requested a book on this subject so that the many souls now awakening would have simple directives to assist them. They desired to show the process of Cosmic Telepathy within the physical brain, what telepathic action is, and how it operates as a "bridge over troubled waters" of an undisciplined mind.

The Council did not necessarily desire to prepare too scientific a document for a subject so dominated by spiritual foundations, yet hoped, to present facts in a simple manner for the benefit of those who seek this direction. They held forth that it would be simply phrased while presenting technical details blended to spiritual overtones of highest importance. They have asked for guided studies, especially helpful for group work, presented in the slightest hint of a textbook format.

They did not desire it to be too technical, yet presented in a more factual manner than most writings on the subject.

The outstanding theme of the hundreds of letters that cross my desk is a request to be told how that individual might pursue this great spiritual adventure. This volume, then, becomes my broad reply to all who have thus written. Those eager to learn will appreciate explanations that are easy to understand. Our dear Commander Hatonn has stated that this book, unlike the others, IS intended for the masses, and will enjoy a mass distribution.

As I prepare this first page, the completed manuscript exists only in the etheric. My human hands and brain must be the catalyst to fuse it together and bring it into manifestation in the physical octave. I gladly dedicate my human energies to do this, knowing that Divine energy will supplement my own one-hundredfold.

Beloved seeker, heaven calls you to experience the DELIB-ERATE SOLITUDE, to... "Be still...and KNOW!"

—Tuella

About The Author—Tuella

Tuella's "calling" as a Messenger of Light began in the early seventies with her channeling work commissioned personally by Ashtar on behalf of the Intergalactic Space Confederation. In addition to *Project World Evacuation*, her future works to be published by Inner Light include *Messengers For The Coming Decade*, *Ashtar—A Tribute*, *On Earth Assignment*, and *The Dynamics of Cosmic Telepathy*.

Introduction

The contents of this book have been spiritually designed in a geometric pattern of twelve for explicit reasons. Twelve is the sum of the etheric whole. It is the completion of all that holds true within the twelve inner planes of reality.

These pages will unfold to those who discover them, the ultimate communications system of all worlds. The force of telepathic thought is a magnetic force which pulls into itself and sends forth from itself the universal atomic structure of creation. The Mind is the Builder, the thoughts are the building material. Thoughts are catapulted into words, ideas or pictures at your level of reception. Limited though they may be, words are tools of convenience used to describe the energies set into motion by a thought transmitted to the receiver.

The art of cosmic telepathy is as old as creation itself. Older, only in sequence, are the symbols of reality that preceded it. From the original symbols of communication, thought went forth to forge its own pathway in the worlds of God's creation.

As humanity returns to the fullness of the stature of MAN, God's creation will master once again the Universal Language of thought transference, through the action of mind.

To herald this time of unfoldment, we release these messages to shed forth understanding and Light into this area of human consciousness. The greatest need of the Bearers of Light and those who work with humanity in the coming crisis will be proficiency in the quality of cosmic communications. That hour could come upon the planet when communications will be the lifeline of survival or rescue.

It is our intent to do all that can be done to assist in this matter by placing into the hands of those who desire to sharpen their mental ability, another tool for instruction.

Blazing a trail for better understanding by using simple diagrams and elementary terminology, we hope to resolve the debris of mystery and ignorance from what should be accepted as normal expression for children of the Creator.

The general consensus of opinion by those who can only be called ignorant is that a human being is delegated to the physical world and that all that is visible or physically attainable is the only goal of having lived upon this planet. Nevertheless, Light has been consistently and increasingly released into the vortex of Earth for the express purpose of piercing such dark mentalities with an understanding of spiritual concepts that lift human life to its highest plane.

By the help of the Invisible World of an entire solar system of Spiritual Leaders who administer the Divine Government of your planet from the Great Tribunals, the Earth is constantly bombarded with rays and influences that bring understanding to man's sense of personal worth, an awareness of his potential for greatness, and his ultimate spiritual goal in having entered the dimension at all.

Included in this tremendous input of possible spiritual attainment is the inherent ability to communicate with his Creator and those of other dimensions who serve His Light. This very natural phenomenon is being brought to the attention of the public at this point in time, to quicken the hearts of those who are destined to find this fulfillment.

Cosmic Telepathy is the inheritance of the Child of Light. It is the resonating force of illumined Mind, piercing the etheric faster than the speed of Light. It is that power delineated to Man, on Earth or wherever he might be. Universal fellowship is a reality without limitation. Limitation is only made possible by belief in its existence.

We call for the awakening of the sleeping genius within Man to awaken and recognize the Father's image within him. Herein lies deliverance from all limitation and thus, the full potential of Mind will be released to God's Will. Mind's physical counterpart already exists in the unknown 85% portion of his brain. The world is waiting for the men and women who are ready to become all that they are capable of being, in the midst of ignorance run rampant. Awake, thou that sleepest, and the Lord Himself shall give thee Light!

Gather yourselves together to consider these classic concepts. Your human effort thus invested will be rewarded by the presence and the response of the Hosts of Heaven.

—Ashtar

Part I
Desire

I
The Dynamics of
Mind Potential

1. The Law of Revelation is a Universal Principle. It has been written, "...if any man lack wisdom, let him ask of God." The Deity has admonished us to "...Ask Me of things to come concerning my sons." Again, we have been told, "Command ye me." Simplest of all these profundities is that promise which states, "Ask...and ye shall receive!" This is the Law of Revelation.

2. Since all is mind, man has but to tune in to any particular mind to *become* that mind with which he shall identify himself. There is nothing man cannot know! As we tune in to the God-Mind through our own Godhead, all things which we seek can be revealed, as needed and divinely permitted. I have great respect for that concept which quietly asserts that "what you can conceive you can achieve." For many years there hung upon the wall of my study a little postcard-sized motto imprinted with this bit of wisdom: "Everything necessary to the solution of any problem is in Universal Mind."

3. Man is of the greater Cosmos—much more than an isolated creature on this planet. The same creative Force that fashioned the galaxies and the universes glows through humanity. You are one of the many manifestations of the energy of creation—Life—identical to all other creation. You ape the universe. As we endeavor to resolve the enigma of Cosmic Forces that ever flow within us in the exploration of ourselves, we simultaneously add to our understanding of the *Reality* of ourselves.

Our generation can never be expressive enough in our gratitude for the great storehouse of wisdom that has been shared with us by George Adamski. His words relative to the subject under study are so vibrant and relevant, they beg to be included here:

4. "There is only one true universal language—the invisible, creative, feeling impulse which is Cosmic Intelligence, flowing as Cosmic Force through all manifestation. This Cosmic Cause, or Universal Force, is ever in motion. It must, of necessity, act upon, or transfer itself from, one subject to another. So the feeling impulse which we call mental telepathy IS the great universal language.

"The study of telepathy will in no way interfere with, or contradict, any religious belief one may have, for telepathy is not a religion, but a Universal Law. Knowledge of this law will give one a greater understanding of self and of the relationship to the cosmos in which we live. Telepathy is the natural ability inherent within all forms of life to communicate their feelings to all other forms. Man is thought in action.

"Every atom in the universe speaks the cosmic language and is capable of communicating with every other atom. Cosmic matter lends itself impartially to all manifestations.

5. "We must admit a universal medium to thought transmission. Mind permeates all space and substance. Mind is composed of highly-charged particles like concentrated substance composing material forms. Only by means of a relay can energy be carried from place to place. Thought is chemical action. Energy of any kind cannot be destroyed. Thought, being a type of energy, will travel through space until it is put to some use. The undeveloped mind rejects all that is not familiar, and retains only those thoughts which confirm the opinions

that mind has already formed."

As I personally studied and meditated upon these words of this great Master, I was given the following message from a member of the Angelic Kingdom. Whether it will bring understanding or confusion remains to be seen. Nevertheless, I do share it with you for your additional thoughts on the matter:

"All That Is"

All that is, is everywhere—boundless, limitless.

All is everything that is; therefore, it is indefinable, immeasurable.

All that is, is a propeller and maintainer of form, but is without form. It is all encompassing. Therefore, nothing that is, escapes its influence and penetration.

All that is, is at every location and every avenue of seeming space between those locations. It is everything and anything filling the void between those locations.

6. The Omnipotent, Omnipresent, Omniscient, Omni-universal Force propels out from within the vortex of its Source—the One Force—the unified energy of All that is.

Passive reception of this Force flows as a process of penetration through the human electromagnetic field into the tensor center of the brain, producing thought in whatever form.

In the active propulsion of this force, the reverse process applies. The outreach of tensor-projected thought, pressing a mental pattern through the personal forcefield, invades the realm of creation from Universal Mind, or Force. Thus, thoughts are—or do become—*things!*"

● ● ●

Our beloved friend, Ashtar, Commander of the Guardian fleets present in our hemisphere, has expressed some justifiable concern for those to whom these various spiritual messages from other dimensions and the concept of cosmic telepathy in general, could create negative responses. We who are so familiar with all of these truths tend to forget what it is like to be suddenly exposed to them when one is still in the throes of spiritual underdevelopment. Ashtar speaks to these:

"Perhaps, dear reader, it has never entered your conscious thinking process that one in your dimension can actually communicate with one in higher dimensions through the process of mind to mind thought placement, or telepathy, as it is known. Have you ever seriously considered the possibility of this phenomenon? Can you open your mind to its possibility? Well, then, can we reason together that if it is possible, then it is feasible that some have therefore done so. If some have therefore done so, then it is probable that these messages have been given and received as has been forthrightly stated.

"May we therefore reason further, that if these messages have so been given and received, then man IS capable of higher things than that to which he has hitherto applied his mental abilities. It is an accepted principle that mankind uses but one-fifth of his mental capacities. Why is this so? Is he not further capable of total mental capacity? If not, why not? Earth has programmed its young far too long in an inadequate way, withholding teachings From the toddler until he is a young child, when his mental capacity is ever the same. Previous years of learning are wasted by withholding that learning, when the very young infant is capable of great reasoning power, if you but understood this truism. The inability of the infant to speak audibly is no indication of his mental capacity. In fact, none of you truly need words at all if you would develop the mind to a fuller capacity.

"We have taught those who thus "hear" us, through long and tedious training sessions of sitting quietly with us, to become receivers of our transmissions. With some such, an ability has to be developed. With others it was present within at birth. Regardless, it is a fact that humankind is perfectly proficient of pure telepathy on the highest level of clarity and perception.

8. "Let us then accept the validity of the process and consider the fruit of it. Our mental conversations with our messengers are as real as your conversations with anyone you know or love or meet. The telepathic thread of experiencing soundless words within the mind is as lucid and fluent as your own tongue. Do you not also know your friends and loved ones on the telephone by the inflections, the vibrations and tones of their voice, as well as the flow of frequency within your being when that familiar voice is heard? So, likewise, do those with whom we are linked in this fashion, also have those corresponding reactions of recognition and response to one who speaks with them telepathically, with a vibrational form of recognition of the validity of the identification given. In most of these instances, this kind of communication comes with ease where old ties exist between the transmitter and the receiver, just as there have doubtless been times when in close association with one greatly beloved, you have known each other's thoughts or the words before they were spoken. All of mankind has known these moments, for the original traits are only idle, not removed.

"So you can agree that our method is a valid one; therefore, can you not accept that we are who we say we are and are capable of speaking with you also, and that our identities are true? Ponder on this and do not reject simply because you do not understand or because of unaccustomedness to the presentation. Consider that with God all things are possible. Your researchers have proven that distance, however great it may be, has no effect upon the communication of mind with mind. The power of thought is said to have no limitations or boundaries. Can you build a wall around the thought of a man? You know that you cannot. Thought is as expansive as the universe itself. Therefore, still the body, quiet the mind, and think on us, and we will respond to those who do in love turn thoughts toward us of the intergalactic Space Confederation."

At a later time, Commander Ashtar continued with his

thoughts on the book, as given here:

"All men are capable of cosmic communication. All of humanity is mentally endowed sufficiently to manifest the aspects of the fully opened mind. The human brain is fully adequate to operate in all of its capacity and in all of its inherent functions of sensory perceptions beyond that of the physical senses. There is no paradox here. There is no mystery involved. We are discussing a natural phenomenon not in any way religious, nor superstitious, nor that which must be hidden in the archives of old philosophies. This natural ability is within the scope of all mankind, and not merely by a gifted few.

"The inability of humanity to exercise these divine talents lies in their own misguided concepts and not in their limitations. All of mind is placed at their disposal, requiring only conscious cooperation of the human consciousness.

"The spiritual essence of soul-mind is the key to realization of the fullest potential within the human lifespan. Mentally speaking, mankind is still crawling on all fours, when they are capable of walking tall in the gait of the conqueror. The awakening of the resonating center of the human brain could deliver the earthean society from self-imposed limitations, if they would but apply themselves to these concepts.

"It is an anachronism that in the days of the earth's beginnings, all of these experiences were a part of daily existence, but time and tides in the evolution of men have washed them away. The call reverberates once again for the restoration of human dignity and the upliftment of man into the reality of his Divine Image and His Divine Birthright.

11. "Furthermore, much is yet to come to pass upon the planet which will necessitate the use of the fullest cosmic awareness in the turbulence of events that can befall this planet. Those who are attuned to Universal Forces will experience their own deliverance through cosmic assistance from the flow of interdimensional communication.

"We pray that the people of Earth will seriously undertake

the return to their spiritual inheritance and their true identity in the higher area of consciousness, and diligently apply themselves to throwing off the slothfulness of the materialistic thought forms. Arise from the sleep of death and reach for the Life that flows unhindered throughout the universe. This is the call that now comes, and may the Eartheans answer quickly and willingly and set in motion this quest for full spiritual participation in the cosmic language of the universe."

• • •

We were first introduced to the word "telepathy" by Mr. Meyers. In speaking for the Psychical Research in 1885, he stated, "We venture to introduce the word 'telepathy,' to cover all cases of impressions received at a distance without the normal operation of the recognized sense organs." In 1927, the scientific community finally dared to incorporate such research into the university level. In ages past, due to bigotry and ignorance, its practice was attributed to black magic or witchcraft, in spite of scriptures filled with such instances. Presently, however, through modern research and experiments on an international scale, telepathy has been proven to be a definite fact. Astronaut Edgar Mitchell is one who combines a keen technical background with an intense curiosity about philosophy. His impression of the relationship of science to philosophy is admirable. He insists that "The two disciplines do not merely coexist, I am completely unable to separate science from art, or from humanities or theology; it's all one big kettle of fish."

12. In the incredible book, *Star Wards*, compiled by spiritual messenger Richard Miller, Monka, our beloved protector of Earth, speaks of men and women who have come to us from the stars. schooled in the use of the mind, to help us learn the techniques and dimensions of our minds so that we can emerge to build and nourish a great new age. Foreseeing the needs of that coming day when the earth will be renewed, "...the minds of MAN are reaching forth to you now so that in your new

world will be incorporated the noblest and finest of all thought."

Monka continues: "In your present time, men and women worship their accomplishments and relegate the knowledge of space and time to the background of their awareness or disregard such thoughts entirely. You have made a fetish of civilization, overwhelmed by your fabrications of stone and steel. Fashioning your own gods, you have forgotten how infinitesimal, how impermanent, and how ignorant you really are.

"Your mind can teach you that even though your bodies remain on earth, of which they are a part, there is a power and a spirit and an awareness of self with which you may become at One with the Symphony of the Creator."

12. "If the Infinite had not desired men to become wise, they would not possess minds—minds that are perceptive and can grasp, in part at least, the immensity of the outer universe. MAN calls from the stars to men, so that they may be comrades together in their use of the questing mind. Men are called to join a fraternity of thought so that their awareness may be expanded."

Think on These Things

1. Define the Law of Revelation.
2. Discuss your understanding of Universal Mind.
3. What is man's relationship to the Universe?
4. Name the Universal Language.
5. What is the Universal Medium for thought transmission?
6. What is the One Force sometimes called?
7. What is the mental capacity of man?
8. List your experiences of telepathy?
9. (a) Do you need to answer the phone to know who is calling?
   (b) Do you need to look at the clock to know the hour?
10. What are the limitations of Cosmic Telepathy?
11. Name one practical reason for interdimensional communication at this point in time?
12. Explain the difference between MAN and human.

NOTES:

II
The Dynamics of
Inspired Enthusiasm

1. The Great Master has said, "He that believeth on me, from within him shall flow rivers of living water" (St. John 7:38). This utterance has always spawned a great enthusiasm within me to press ever onward for greater and greater things, to realize that we do indeed go from glory unto glory as we walk with God, marching triumphantly to unlimited frontiers. We remember that it has been said that all of God's limitations are within us. Therefore, let us arise to a sense of spiritual endowment and truly seek our inner splendor. I am saying, my friend, that there is a place for a divine sense of extravagant enthusiasm as we follow the leadings, the quest for spiritual attainment!

2. I never tire of quoting Betty White's Invisibles, who stated: "Walk through your days as a creature with folded wings, conscious of the possession of another dimension and the ability to enter it." A divinity unfolds within us and we will ultimately remember and pull through our human consciousness all the things we knew before. Truth becomes an echo, and this incarnation will unfold in a natural way.

3. So we go with gusto down this pilgrim pathway. Truly, enthusiasm is a mark of spiritual well-being. Our "venture inward" is a joyous, wonderful adventure. Believe in the

enthusiasm of an *Abundant Life*. Refuse mediocrity! Refuse boredom and deadness! Refuse apathy—it is spiritual and emotional death! Yield not to the temptation, "I'll *believe* it when I *see* it;" rather, declare energetically, "When I *believe* it, I will *see* it!"

We all desire to share and to be a blessing to others, yet how well we know we cannot teach unless we ourselves are taught. We must be filled to overflowing ourselves if we would teach another, and then, how beautifully it pours from out of the overflow!

I share with you here a message that was received many many years ago, yet it is relevant within this context:

"If we are to understand with our infinitely small understanding the origin of worlds, surely we must first understand the origin of ourselves. For were not at first all the 'sons of God' rejoicing with Him at the hour of other creations? The call of the universe is for a soul to know itself! To sense its total beingness, to respond and draw upon its inner strength. We fail if we do not begin at this beginning."

4. "The cataclysmic event of soul awareness unfolds like the petals of a flower to the sun, With infinite detail each petal slowly lowers, unfolds, lengthens and spreads itself, absorbing and reflecting more and more of its hidden beauty. Just so it is within the soul of one who seeks and finds a response from spirit in the devotional life. Every area of the life is touched by and affected by that touch from Spirit."

5. "The permeation of cosmic force throughout life, yea, even the body, affects all the contacts, all the problems, the goals, the attributes of the earth life. Here, now, is the beginning of polarity—or spark, if you please—which releases the power of God. *Power from God is that indescribable ability to simply stand as conqueror in the midst of all earth life's situations!* It inhibits the forces of darkness and releases the Light of heaven wherever one chooses to send it. This is the Healing Light, the Delivering Light, the Catastrophic Light which can

change the tides in the affairs of men, of nations and worlds. This Light encases the child of God and becomes not only a shield of defensive protection, but an offensive outflow as well. Here, again, is the alternating effect of the positive and negative effect within electrical power. It goes out as it should; it comes in as it should, and together, constitutes a reservoir of Cosmic Force."

Perhaps, dear one, you may feel that our momentum has begun too slowly in getting on with our subject of cosmic telepathy. Please know that the pace is deliberate, because time must be taken to build SURE SPIRITUAL FOUNDATIONS before you venture into the invisible world. The encasement of Light mentioned above is a vital part of earlier preparation in your quest.

7. The Masters have called this text "a vastly organized bombardment of truth." Believe me, beloved, it is organized with a distinct pattern in mind, and each chapter follows another in the divine order of things, for specific purposes. The first section—the first four chapters of the book—are for that purpose of building the foursquare foundation of right desire before taking you into the disciplines that follow.

8. Commander Ashtar has spoken through another of "the tremendous need to establish a contact with your Godhead! He asserts that no power on earth or from any realm outside the earth can harm one who dwells in perfect accord with his higher Self."

9. & 10. It is important to understand that the development of a soul is of God and not of man. It is a spiritual work and not a fleshly one. The Mind itself is that fragment of God within us through which divinity flows. Also, consider that soul development and resulting awareness is a very natural process. The plateau of Soul/Mind activity awaits all who diligently and enthusiastically, as well as *patiently*, apply themselves. Finally, we can add to these thoughts the fact that the spiritual development of a soul is the work of *many*. That one

who would attain has many unseen helpers—Beautiful, Shining, Wise Ones who minister to our lifestreams and guard our pathway!

11. My friend, there was a time in my own life when "I walked this sod, a thankless clod," without a glimmer of Light across my pathway, or so it seemed. But in the darkest hour of my life, "there stood a man beside me." His name was Jesus! I had found a friend! I learned to love my new Friend, because I knew He loved me. Timidly, I began to walk beside Him. I began to quietly tell people what a wonderful Friend He was. In this encounter, the grass became greener, the trees taller. I found that I could talk to the oak trees and the strawberry plants. I was *alive!* The whole universe seemed to flow through my being. I felt at one with the ant that crawled across my foot. I found that my whole body was a receiving set. My Love and my Thought World and the very hairs on my head were antennae, and I was one with every other life form in the universe! It was more than wonderful... it was *incredible!*

And so it is, I become excited about Divine Possibilities that are in store for all of us. I hope that you will, also. Dear one, I am talking about *INSPIRED ENTHUSIASM:* It, too, is vital in the dynamics of cosmic telepathy.

Think on These Things

1. Where are the limitations of God to be found?
2. Is the pursuit of knowledge wasted by physical death?
3. What is the Abundant Life?
4. Describe the unfoldment of Spiritual Awareness.
5. Define Spiritual Power.
6. Why is a sure Spiritual Foundation important to approaching Cosmic Telepathy?
7. Discuss "right desire."
8. How do you establish a contact with your Godhead?
9. Can we "develop" ourselves?
10. Give three reasons for your reply.
11. Describe your own Awakening to the Universe.
12. Why is enthusiasm a Spiritual Attitude?

NOTES:

III
The Dynamics of
Desire Power

1. & 2. Thought, with the added ingredient of feeling, creates *desire power.* The intensity of emotion releases the charge force of power within us from whatever dimension it may originate. The Teachers have said, "Our thoughts wend their way over vast distances to settle in the mind of one who has reached energetically and enthusiastically for our words. Great desire and dedication, combined with the intention to use the information for the Light and the coming Kingdom, are the ingredients which pull our thoughts to that one who would receive them. No one will be ignored who opens his mind freely and in love, to receive from the Heavenly Host."

Through one who must remain anonymous, Cosmic Master Aljanon has sent us this message: "A thought plus an emotion equals a feeling. Feeling is the accumulation of the energy force combined with the stamp of the individual's consciousness and allowed to be released upon the world and his body. What occurs on the world level?"

3. "Every thought, as you are well aware, is energy, pure and simple, and as such, it has force—the force of the individual's will, which sends it forth."

4. The Invisible Teachers who spoke through Betty White a generation ago put it beautifully: "The energy with which

you demand of us will be the measure of what you will get." Not so much the energy of demand as a showing of force that calls *for its complement,* energy measure for measure." They tell us that we need to "put strength into that first dead lift" while keeping relaxed, and to "stimulate the spirit to respond with great wonder." We need to unstopper what Raynor Johnson called the Inner Splendor, to let it rise, letting the heart dominate, yet "holding yourself together around a good firm core of aspiration."

5. The desire of your heart is more important to you than the desire of your mind. The preparation of your soul is by far of greater importance than your mental preparation. They tell us, "As soon as you have yourself in the right condition, we can come." We must arouse ourselves; they cannot do it for us. The celestial inspirational forces come to us, seek us out, from a combination of conditions that we create ourselves. Our own soul yearning emanations and charge force unites with heavenly forces to encourage a mutual exchange between heaven and earth. We are not to be overcome with thoughts of what we are going to receive, only to believe in the legitimate ambition of the attainability of higher powers opening within us. The Teachers have stated, "Love is the powerful medium of communication, the stepping stone which brings us safely across." Thus we see that the process of cosmic telepathy is propagated through mutual desire. Other-dimensional beings stand ready to speak with us, awaiting only a relaxed readiness on our part.

We have learned that there are three kinds of telepathy: that transferring from solar plexus to solar plexus; that which is directly sent and received mind to mind; and that which is the resonating energy from soul to soul. In a communication from a being called Latrob to Jacques Drabier, this was explained:

6. "Solar plexus communication occurring between ordinary and emotional people is governed by desire and primarily

centered in the animal and astral bodies. Mind to mind telepathy is void of all emotional conditions, with no desire to get the message through, but passive in nature. (Concern over whether or not you will succeed can block your energy sent out to where *it will act as a boomerang and return to its sender).* At the same time, a receiver who is too intense in the sending releases large amounts of energy which tend to block the *incoming* flow. To truly comprehend telepathy, one needs to learn the nature of force, of emanations and radiations of energy currents."

7. The highest form of telepathy is from soul to soul. It is only possible where an integrated personality has the ability to focus in the soul consciousness. The work of telepathic communicators is one of the most important as the New Age dawns. It will be of immense value to anyone to learn and study the significance of this form of contact."

The least desire on the part of any recipient will flood forth an ocean of willingness from higher dimensions to respond to that desire. In communication there is always a purpose, a common denominator which sets up reciprocal vibrations. These in turn become avenues of communication. The telepathic journey is ever waiting, but few there are who are ready to enter its unknown paths. We tap the source of supply of these energies in our contact with God and Higher Consciousness! Someone has said, "reach as high as you can, and tie a knot and hang on." Let us ever realize that existence is not creation, and contact is not destination. Also, our energy and power must be conserved, renewed, an inner assurance of stability, independent of outward circumstances; to realize we "possess a feeling of strength beyond our own, accessible and usable."

The flow of our contact need not be a trickle, sparse and hampered. The receiving is limited only by our desire power and the energy to back it up. Our Source is inexhaustible, sympathetic and understanding, unstinted in the giving of all that is good for us, that we have earned and deserve, but only provided we desire to give it away after we get it.

1. Have you heard the little story of the three little goldfish who swam round and round in a circle in their little bowl? One day their caretaker, taking pity on their crowded and limited space, put them into a lovely, large round bowl. Strangely enough, the little goldfish continued to swim in the same circle of circumference to which they were accustomed. Then there was the lazy rooster who waited for others to crow at the dawn of the new day, and then he would just nod his head! Desire power will determine what you accomplish in your devotional life and this telepathic life force.

2. & 3. Once again, in an endeavor to stimulate our planetary thinking on the profound teachings of George Adamski, we are attentive to his words concerning the awesome force: "Universal Force has two fields of action—attraction and repulsion—which transform into energy. In mechanical fields, force is recognized as energy; in psychological fields, as thought. Thought is a chemical action."

3. "We know that a law of affinity exists, with attracting and repelling actions which command the combination of chemicals to create a form of energy. It is an aggressive force, radiating in all directions, causing pressure on surrounding force-space to create waves in that element. Thought is not sent out in one straight line, but in billions of straight lines in all directions, like a radiating spark of light extending in equal force in all directions. Mind is the medium with which thought is carried from one point to another."

8. "Space is a sea of activated, attracting and repelling force, always in motion. All motion is made up of tiny units we call atoms. An atom may be compared to a miniature solar system containing a central sun around which, in definite orbits, revolve negative electrical charges, or units of force. The central sun, or nucleus of the atom, is a positive charge equaling perfectly the total number of electrical charges around it.

Miniature universes carry an indelible memory of their existence in each manifestation. Manifestation is born out of potential force which, through the law of affinity, forces the particles to unite."

9. Let us look to our Heavenly Father, who giveth all wisdom, for an understanding of all these wonders of His creation. Master Kuthumi promises us that help. "In daring to release a volume of this nature from the Hierarchy, we unanimously place our blessings on all souls who desire to find this fulfillment in their life. Souls will be helped by direct influence from the highest planes, to find a true path of self-realization and understanding of their Godness. Our blessings placed upon it will expand the outreach, the influence, and successful application."

As this book progressed I asked Master Kuthumi to discuss the relationship of spiritual attainment to clear and valid telepathy. He responded:

10. "Telepathy is an impersonal, universal principle. It brings to mind another principle stating 'like attracts like,' as well as the law of vibrations. As you are, so you will attract. It is active and present, whatever level of evolvement is attained."

"If it is the desire of the seeker to maintain communication from the uppermost level and the highest spiritual realm, then it behooves that one to seek to live the most spiritual life that is possible for them at their level of attainment. It literally means walking in all of the Light that you have received. It is *living* your Light that makes it your own and a part of you, impregnated into all levels of Being. It means conquering every challenge your Light (understanding) has given you, so that you can be readied for more knowledge and advancement to life on an even higher plane. *Light is not truly your own until you have produced its action in your life!*"

10. "One cannot be slothful in spiritual attainments and expect to receive back through the superconscious mind, contacts from the highest and worthiest levels. As a man is, so will

he attract to himself—this is the law of attraction. Where you are on the pathway, that is the nature you will attract to yourself. Spiritual attainment is vitally related to the quality of the telepathic communication that will feed back to the seeking mind. One must realize that telepathic ability is always present—even in the animal kingdom!"

I was also interested in his opinion concerning the rather controversial question about the advisability of beginners practicing this attunement alone or in groups, and this explanation was forthcoming:

11. "This, again, is directly related to the soul involved. It is always safe for any soul to attune to the highest level of contact when alone, as long as they have mastered the basic principles of Light and the use of that Light. They must have attained to a spiritual discernment capable of a distinction of the Light from the darker interrupting forces. They must have attained a spiritual stance that assures them of their protection so that fear does not enter the exercise. Fear in any degree will attract that which is feared. A strong cocoon of love energy is vital."

"The rank beginner, not studied in these areas and one who is not evolved in any way, who would sit down to open his being, would attract to him from the astral level those equivalent to his attainment, attaching to his Being unwelcome sources of information. So here, again, there must be first an attunement with the Source of all Creation and the God Presence *within*, to assure quality in the contact. Quality is, of course, discerned by examining content."

"There must first be a spiritual soul power, an opening of the heart with Love to God and all of His Creation. This flow of Love is the finest protection there is. Anyone covered by Light and filled with the Love vibration, faces no danger in telepathic communications with the higher levels. A group setting would therefore be a safer background for one who is untutored in spiritual concepts. But one who has walked with God and loved his fellowman will not in any way be harmed in his solitude by practicing his meditation and cosmic telepathy alone."

The response within my own Being to his words is a familiar one:

The Lord is my shepherd: I shall not want.

He maketh me to lie down in green pastures: he leadeth me beside the still waters.

He restoreth my soul: he leadeth me in the paths of righteousness for his name's sake.

Yea, though I walk through the valley of the shadow of death, I will fear no evil: for thou art with me; thy rod and thy staff they comfort me.

Thou preparest a table before me in the presence of mine enemies: thou anointest my head with oil; my cup runneth over. Surely goodness and mercy shall follow me all the days of my life: and I will dwell in the house of the Lord forever.

—PSALM 23

Think on These Things

1. Define "desire power."
2. How are the thoughts of our Space Brothers attracted to us?
3. What is thought?
4. How do you measure the energy that will be received?
5. How do you build your Spiritual Foundation?
6. State the three kinds of Telepathy.
7. Describe the highest telepathy.
8. What is the "Awesome Force"?
9. Discuss self-realization.
10. Explain the Law of Attraction.
11. Why is fear a destructive emotion?
12. Define spiritual attunement, and explain its relationship to Cosmic Telepathy.

NOTES:

IV
The Dynamics of Commitment

1. & 2. Our desire and enthusiasm for this spiritual endeavor will stagnate if it is not focused to definite ends through a dedicated commitment. Too speedily developing in this matter would produce a confusion of efforts resulting more in chaos than character. Unless the mind is properly prepared to receive, the content—like chaff—falls upon rocky soil. Contact is not destination. It is not so much the receiving that is uppermost as is the ability to accept, understand and absorb that which is given. There is a deep purpose in all telepathic efforts with the etheric realms. That purpose is never one of frivolity or entertainment. Truths are needed by others to advance themselves. The equipment for advancement is truth. Truth lived and absorbed into the earth life becomes the armor of achievement on this physical plane.

All cosmic telepathic endeavor should be entered into in the attitude of dedication to service to humanity. Without this dedication, the accent on morality and character-building would lose its force.

2. The maintenance of an attitude of desire and flexibility is adequate for a beginner to receive response, the desire being for truth and personal growth, and not for the sensational fruits of phenomena. Our beautiful Heavenly Forces spend

long periods of time and much energy in preparation of a soul for ultimate telepathic contact. It becomes very frustrating to them when the awakening is perverted into wrong channels for wrong purposes. One Speaker has contributed this thought: "The lethargic soul is greatly hindering his progression after death by taking no thought to eternal things while upon the earth plane. Life on planet Earth is intended to be a preparatory period, during which one must face and overcome many obstacles and handicaps, yet leave the earth scene some contribution for the good of the whole. Primarily, the purpose of embodiment is the advancement and development of character and divine purpose. This is each one's duty to himself; to be able in that day to look upon the deeds of this life with a feeling of *pride* and a sense of accomplishment of purpose. True that one may very well pass this way again; that is true, but the future passing will be all the easier and all the greater for the success of the present one well done."

3. Consider also that physical embodiment produces a kind of human separation and therefore, loneliness. This enables each one of us to develop an individual character, but until the ego becomes aware of this, it seeks escape in the crowd. Yet only by becoming still more lonely will we become less lonely. For we must go still farther into the center of Being until we feel enwrapped by that consciousness of unity with the Creator. Escape from our inescapable aching void is not effected by external activities, but by going into what seems to be still greater solitude.

In discussing this spirit of commitment, Andromeda Rex has made this comment: "For this we ever watch and monitor your world, seeking those hearts that are awakening to the greater picture, and the greater burden for a planet and its people; those who speak of the needs of this world in their prayers and calls; those whose hearts bleed for the needs of humanity. This kind of devotion to the Kingdom of God on Earth registers our attention automatically." Thus we understand that inspiration comes for definite production. Oil flows into emptied vessels. Inspiration must have a container. It fills what is prepared for it. The flow must push something in a practical manner.

• • •

During my own earlier days of sitting with the Masters for instruction, which included cosmic telepathic efforts, I received a most interesting discourse that reveals a pattern of procedure in their assistance to the beginner. I am sure you will enjoy reading it:

"All of us use a certain system in assisting the disciple on the pathway in unfolding awareness. (1) First, we lead the soul through its curiosity pursuit or the initial beginnings of telepathic exercise. (2) Then we satisfy its many many personal questions and needs. (3) Then we withdraw for a period to allow the soul to turn its attention to mental preparation, to feed the mind with knowledge and understanding (books, lectures, conferences). (4) Then, we seek to concentrate attention upon personal growth and development for broader use of contact. (5) Ultimately, when these preliminary stages are completed, we then approach the soul once more with the divine purpose. The purpose of all higher contact is always to call upon mortals to consider the fact of spirit survival and to intelligently prepare for it with growth and understanding toward that end; and to sense the personal destiny in the incarnation; and finally, to experience a deeper understanding of the greater cosmos and man's relationship to all creation in all of the universal planes of existence. This is *always* the message, and when *it* is totally absorbed by the human contact, then they are ready to teach others."

As I analyzed these five simple steps, I came up with six breakdowns within the pattern that helped me to understand it, as follows:

5. (1.) **CURIOSITY**—Lesser teachers hold the attention

of the student at any cost—any method—contact and not content is the issue here. Much trivia and irrelevancy present as student learns to listen.

(2.) CONVICTION—Through seeking much earthly and personal information, the muddy waters of trivia begin to clear, still with a strong mixture of false and truth, until discernment takes over, while keeping pace with new revelation. Insatiable hunger for books, lectures, and like-minded people.

(3.) CONCENTRATION—Messages begin to depart the personal level and approach the character level, becoming more spiritual, more dependable, from higher sources.

(4.) CONSECRATION—At this point, soul memory is triggered, fear is dispelled, desire to truly serve is awakened as messages enter greater depth of truth and wisdom.

(5.) COMMISSION—A certain and sure gift becomes distinctly present for the mission that soul has in service to the world. The Hierarchal Sponsoring Master is revealed or identified.

(6.) COMMITMENT—Here a sense of mission, even perhaps an awareness of its nature, flows into the soul along with the call, "Follow Me!"

Perhaps the procedure is a bit reminiscent of a cool plunge into the lake when first one lowers the big toe into the water; then, more adventurously, gets in up to the knees; then finally, deliberately dives in!

• • •

6. Who is there among us who did not at first feel they just could not find the time for these things—for that early morning vigil or that late night tuning in? Yet finally we did learn it was only possible by making the time! It is not the application to necessary details of life, but the unbroken application, that makes a life commonplace!

From the Speakers have come these words: "The secular things are needful, but the spiritual things are vital issues of life, and it is within these commodities we labor for mankind. The performance of the daily tasks is sanctified and uplifted all the day by one hour spent in cosmic telepathic exercise with the Etheric Worlds. The consequence of an ounce of faithfulness to this end cannot be calculated by living souls on the planet."

7. For our continuing inflow, we need to constantly practice the higher consciousness actively in our daily lives. We need to develop a rhinoceros hide for the rough and tumble, the unsympathetic and thwarting contacts of life.

I spent some years on a Texas cattle ranch, an enormous one! My nearest neighbors were hundreds of Hereford cattle whose tremendous drinking trough was just outside my kitchen window, beyond the fence. I have never forgotten the lesson that trough taught me. I watched the cows drink deeply of the water and would see it pour out of the faucet as it lowered its level, ever filling, ever flowing as long as they drank from it. Then at times, in the midday hot sun, no cattle would be present. The faucet would be stilled, the water would cover over with dust and debris, heated from the sun, *because there was no outflow to replenish the inflow!* And so it is, that in our spiritual pilgrimage we must maintain a flow by pouring out our truth, rather than stealing a cup for ourselves and running with it. We can get rid of the stoppage at the point of contact with the world, as opportunity is given and guidance is present. Except for periods for rest, or when nervous tension is present, our spiritual activity is always toward continuous flow.

8. Our Father is Love. We are most like God when acting in reflection of that Love, speaking in Love, handling situations with Love, living an attitude of Love. This insures the continuing inflow of Love to us.

Andromeda Rex has said, "Love is the strongest element in the universe and the highest possible vibration on your planet. It shines upon our monitoring board like diamonds across a dark sky. Love builds a road, so to speak, along which our communications can travel back to that source of thought which has been projected to us. Thus, as you lift your loving thoughts higher to us, you enable us to return our own along that same energy pathway to you."

To return for a moment to the inspiring words of The Invisibles through Betty White, enjoy this with me:

"The world can sap your strength unconsciously. The absorbing quality of earth life can diminish your supply. Return regularly to the powerhouse. The Source will not desert you unless you lose your surety and *strangle yourself with tensions.* There you cut it off and choke yourself. When you sense depreciation, return to attunement, and it will follow you in the minutiae of work. When traveling full speed ahead, 'trust the stars are still there.' You can look up at them when the night comes. Attuning is a filling of comfort in presenting yourself to a potent security. There make your decisions, and then, go and do them!"

● ● ●

9. Through Yolanda, spiritual messenger for Mark-Age, St. Getmain once emphasized, "We have no need to prove ourselves to you, but you have a need to prove yourselves to us, to show your trustworthiness and your responsibility to be true leaders and true disciples and true inhabitants of this wonderful planet Earth, which is going into its highest state of evolvement."

Master Kuthumi has commented to me, "To rationalize as to whether or not cosmic telepathy is possible for humanity is totally irrelevant. The focus here is upon the willingness to accept the discipline required to try. Criticism comes easy; serious application does not. Strong-hearted, determined souls will forge their way through with an invincible determination that will bring the desired results. The weaker-minded participants will drop off along the way. We look upon and measure the depth of sincerity and the will to enter the pathway of the communicating disciple. Amongst the many new to these truths, this book will 'separate the men from the boys,' as your worldly expression has it, and many new teachers and messengers will begin service to the world and the ongoing Light."

It has been stressed that the acquiring of these mental techniques is directly *in proportion to the effort made to master them*. We must keep up a semblance of discipline to build a strong devotional life. Perseverance and diligence are required to overcome inertia in the spiritual adventure. Ashtar has said through an unknown source, "Be worthy of contact by the etheric forces by being apart from the fleshly pursuits of the world. To be IN the world but not OF the world should be your goal. Meditate upon perfection—upon that which you would change from evil to good, from sickness to health, and from ignorance to understanding. Concentrate upon being a balanced human, for you can be of no real service in an unbalanced condition, to the Space People or to yourself."

10. The more often we expose ourselves to the heavenly encounter, the more our own frequency is elevated and the greater the ease of telepathic communication. George Adamski was told, "Thoughts are received and transmitted in exactly the same way as by radio, along certain wavelengths, but *minus any instrument*. We work directly from brain to brain, and here again, distance is no barrier. However, an open and receptive mind is needed for success. Through all the years you have been sending thoughts to us, we have answered. This has established a *solid cable-like connection* between us by maintaining the thought waves in a single channel. Whenever your mind is open, we can send you the information you require, exactly as you could receive a message over a telephone." His strongest contact, Orthon, revealed, "We had you under observation for some years before I finally contacted you, and we felt sure your knowledge of telepathy would be adequate. At our first meeting I tested your ability to send out and receive telepathic messages. It remained to be seen if and how you

would translate this interest into action, how well you could stand up under the ridicule and skepticism bound to come your way, and whether you would be tempted to use your contacts with us for self aggrandizement or commercialism." These words reveal much to the sincere student of telepathy.

A message to me from a beloved female Commander, in my early training, explained, "Each time you enter our frequency, you are strengthened in it. Whether or not you record at all is unimportant. The blending of our frequencies prepares you for a deeper ministry. Distance has no effect upon our meetings together. Your own desire power is the key to contact. Your form is overshadowed and enshrouded by the Christ Presence when you are in contact with us, and your form appears as light to those in astral vision. The bodies of Light workers must be impregnated with the highest frequencies before our projection can be received in a visible way."

The relationship of the student of Light and his Spiritual Teachers is a very intimate one—not a fact to be bandied about at every social gathering. On the wings of thought their words come as quickly as thought can fly from the heart that calls to the heart that replies. The Space Brothers are here in both physical and etheric form. They are here to supplement, *and not to replace*, our own God Consciousness, our own attunement with our Christ selves and our own communion with the I AM Presence and our Spiritual Teachers. They can do many things with their equipment to awaken and stimulate certain spiritual centers, to help us along the pathway. The time is short, and that is why they come to help humanity. They are in tune with our personal Teachers and our Christ Selves. They can glance down on a whole city and determine the spiritual aspiration of each person, as well as their physical ability to endure any conditioning of the energy forces which might be desired for certain individuals.

11. Their monitoring fills every moment. Other persons who compose the immediate surroundings of a child of Light

are also included in their monitoring, since everything that touches a channel also touches the mission of that channel. Every close human contact or physical association comes under the scrutiny of those who watch over God's channels for the influence that may be willingly or unwillingly touching that lifestream. It is their objective to police the environment of their representatives to remove clutter and confusion as it enters. For the messenger must have freedom to express and to demonstrate in the assigned mission for the Divine Program for the planet. Not only has this permission been given by the messenger in the original commitment, but most often was given even before embodiment. Thus it is the continuing commitment that we do give the Spiritual Overseers of our lives full and complete permission to march through our entire being and world daily and cleanse or remove from them any thing or situation that would interfere or destroy God's Divine Will in our lives. This is the ongoing consecration evidenced in the words of the Apostle who declared, "I die daily."

In the meditation period there are various manifestations that would indicate the onset of telepathic communication. Perhaps you will sense a nearness, or there may be a swaying feeling upon the upper torso, or the fingers may feel a tingling. The reflexes may produce lesser or greater jerky motion as the frequency of a beam is placed into position. There may be a drowsiness, but these are only the evidence of the flesh and its density being quieted for the business at hand. And that business is total relaxation and total receptivity.

11. To the beginner, incessant questions of an earthly nature is a novelty which finally wears off. It is then in response to genuine sincerity that the higher sources enter the communications. The earth forces pull away from concentration on the highest level, which is the secret of all meaningful communication. Your gift cannot be taken away, but it can be buried in debris of the everyday life. A cosmic channel must have an environment that is joyful, with a relaxed state of mind in daily living, for consciousness to be raised to the place where impressions of a universal value will flow naturally. Transmissions can become clouded or the delicate thread of telepathy broken by our unhappiness, a disturbed mind, even electrical atmospheric conditions—fog, mists, and storms. For some reason not completely understood, when the moon is in its negative period or dark side, the telepathic thread does not flow as smoothly as it does during the nine positive days before full moon. Again, a receiving "station" can go stale from physical exhaustion or being tired. Rest refreshes the outlook as well as strengthening the telepathic thread.

Space Commander Anton, formerly stationed at Cook Mountain near Deming, New Mexico, was discussing thought propulsion with me a few months ago. His entire comment is worth repeating here:

"If you will consider that all things in the universe operate on the principle of propulsion and apply it continually to all things, much mystery dissolves and understanding takes its place. The ionization of the atmosphere with units of life and light that compose it, are magnetic particles which form the thread of telepathy between one mind and another. They congeal as thought waves which carry the original thought impulse through space into time and human passivity."

"You have asked me whether there is any pertinent relativity between nearness to a space base location and physical contacts with its occupants. The distance being near *is* primarily a factor in *physical* contacts. A close proximity is much desired in these kinds of contacts. However, where the contact is confined to mental thought transference only, distance is not a factor. More *physical* contacts have occurred in the vicinity of the bases than anywhere else for obvious reasons. Our contactors do not themselves remain long outside of their bases, appearing in an instant to those to whom they have been sent to deliver whatever may be necessary at that moment. Those who have been driven or escorted into the bases have had this occurrence at or near a base area. We do not travel long distances in the physical octave to culminate these things. It is unnecessary."

"Contactors generally form their contacts with one who is comparably near in terms of distances (I do not speak here of cosmic contacts from craft in the etheric above). The primary contactor then facilitates a relay to the contactee, from other sources outside of their perimeter. However, the projection method is also used by the Commanders in reaching their contactees. We, in all cases, radiate our beam upon those who labor with us so that their personal frequency has been greatly elevated for more efficient reception of the thoughts projected to them."

Thus we understand that our personal commitment to the Divine Program of Light for this planet not only brings to us the full cooperation of those who administer it, but opens the door to our own participation in that program.

12. We have concluded the foursquare framework of the firm spiritual foundation upon which to build a strong telepathic link with the highest spiritual forces of the etheric worlds. (1.) We must understand its absolute possibility. (2.) We must experience an enthusiastic attitude and appreciation for all manifestations of life. (3.) The charge force of our own desire power must augment heaven's desire to comply. (4.) Our commitment to the Kindgom of God on earth must be unqualified and complete. With this sound foundation, we can safely proceed into more technical aspects of our subject.

Think on These Things

1. How do we choke off spiritual endeavor?
2. What is the purpose in all telepathic effort?
3. How do we overcome loneliness?
4. How is the potential telepath recognized by the higher commands?
5. What are the six steps in the Hierarchical pattern for a newly-awakened messenger?
6. What makes a life commonplace?
7. How do we maintain the spiritual inflow?
8. When are we most like God?
9. How do we prove ourselves as worthy candidates for telepathic communication?
10. What mental attitude is necessary for telepathy?
11. Discuss the effect of personal environment in the life of a spiritual messenger.
12. List the four factors that form a strong spiritual foundation for Cosmic Telepathy.

NOTES:

Part II
Determination

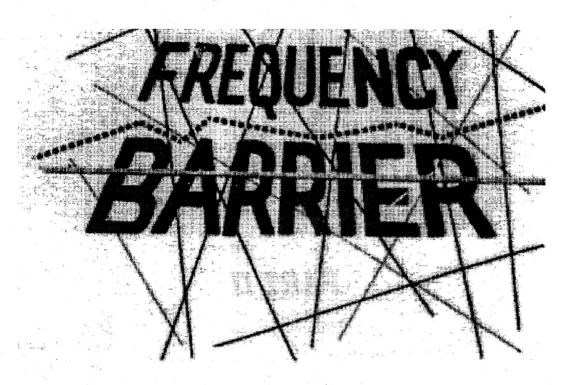

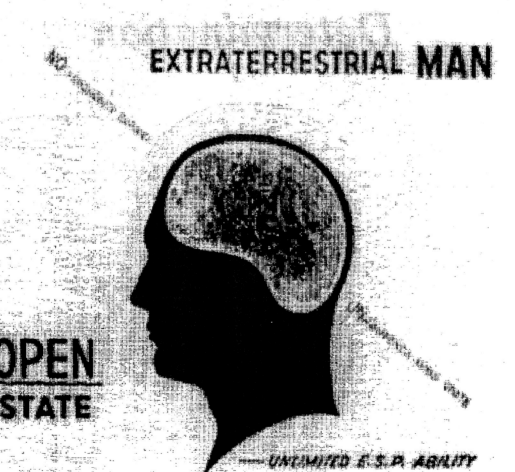

V
The Dynamics of
Frequency

Perhaps we are somewhat tempted to wonder if the frequency of the planet has any relevance whatever to Cosmic Telepathy. I trust that with the completion of this chapter, you will agree with me that the relevance is potent and has, in the past, represented the difference between success and failure. As a body of background information, these few pages concerning the frequency of our planet may broaden the scope of understanding and produce an appreciation for the difficulties with which man has had to cope in the past in expanding spiritual abilities. The dynamics of the planetary frequency are directly related to man's ability to respond in a positive way to the divinity within.

My thoughts along this line were stimulated when a friend passed me a copy of his lecture on "THE FREQUENCY BARRIER." Jacques P. Drabier is a beloved spiritual teacher and popular lecturer from Phoenix, Arizona; a channel, and a serious UFO investigator of many years. His paper dealing with the Mental, or Closed State, Conditions contained challenging food for thought. Fortunately, this gifted brother is also an artist by profession, and his sketches are included along with his provoking words, here quoted verbatim:

1. "An unnatural physical condition has existed on the

earth which has been affecting all life forms upon the planet for a considerable length of time. This unnatural physical condition has been referred to as the 'Frequency Barrier.' We who live on this planet have been totally unaware of this barrier, since none has ever escaped the effects of this unnatural condition to discover that a better, or a natural condition opposite to the frequency barrier, was in existence, until the 1969 Apollo Moon Mission."

2. "One of the reasons the extraterrestrials and their monitoring spacecraft have visited us consistently has been for the purpose of determining a solution to the frequency barrier problem. They are very much aware of the natural conditions of outer space, which gives them a point of reference for comparing the frequency barrier. While observing the effects of the frequency barrier upon themselves, they can evaluate and determine its restrictions upon us from their open mental state (or full use of the brain), for they, too, are human. Now these unnatural effects have gradually diminished, having gradually taken place over the last 26,000 years."

"It is necessary to consider the effects of this barrier upon the life forms of earth. The brain of man (and animals) is bioelectromagnetic in nature. Humanity uses a form of electromagnetism to think. Thoughts are actually electromagnetic signals, using a complex series of synapse circuits within the brain as routes for these signals to stimulate an associated flow of references from the memory bank. These released references are also electromagnetic signals.

3. "The frequency barrier has been affecting the thinking processes of humanity for thousands of years. If humanity had not had to live within the frequency barrier, limiting, hindering, and denying the use of many brain circuits, they would have the same 100 percent mental capabilities as their ancestral relatives from outer space, for the brains of all are exactly alike."

"Everything that exists in the universe has its own vibra-

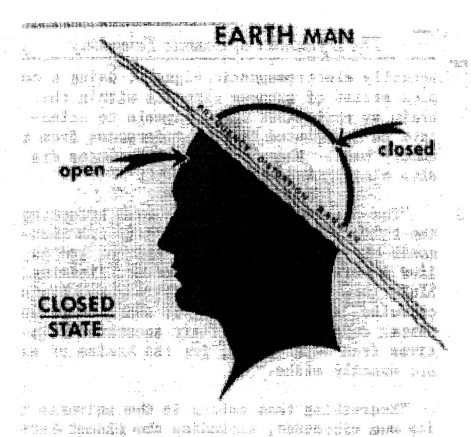

tion, including the planet Earth. All vibrations are electromagnetic. The frequency barrier has been partly produced by the earth's inharmonious vibration with the electromagnetic thinking process of the human brain. Certain key strata layers which are layered upon one another, constituting the physical structure of our planet, have been misaligned, causing the planet to vibrate unnaturally. This planet's electromagnetic vibration may be likened to a radio communications jamming apparatus, which is used to prevent reception and transmission of intelligible signals during wartime."

"The people of this planet have not always been mentally restricted by the frequency barrier. For at a time in the *very* distant past the inhabitants of this planet had the full use of their mental faculties. The beginning of the frequency barrier has been said to have occurred during the time of the great flood, for this was the lowest point in the history of man."

(Readers please note: The forty days of the Great Flood have been associated with the tipping of planet Maldek and the overflow of its oceans upon earth at the time of its destruction.—T.)

"At that time the thinking processes of mankind upon the planet were drastically affected. Man was reduced, over a period of time, by the frequency barrier's influence, to a four-and one-half foot tall, hairy creature we now call Neanderthal Man (Fig. 1), or caveman. The Neanderthal had very few brain channel circuits which would function, due to the frequency barrier. Through earthquake and volcanic activity, partial realignment of earth's internal strata enabled Java Man (Fig. 2) to use more brain channel circuits than did his predecessor. As time passed, more such realignments occurred which gradually (in proportion) decreased the unnatural vibration of the planet itself. The Cro-Magnon Man (Fig. 3) also had less hindrance from the frequency barrier. His time in history was during the Ice Age, when many changes took place both internally and upon the surface of the earth. Evidence of further progress in mental abilities of man occurred in the Egyptian culture (Fig. 4). The Egyptian, as well as the Greek, Aztec, Incan, Mayan, Babylonian, and Assyrian civilizations were all built over fault lines of the earth, where they developed and flourished because of the electromagnetic vibrations which built up in these faults, assisting the minds of the people living over them. These assisting vibrations were temporary, since earthquakes eventually removed the vibrations from these faults. The civilizations without these assisting vibrations in the faults no longer progressed, but rather, started to decline."

"Interestingly enough, the people who visited us from space took precautions against the frequency barrier by setting their craft into a vibrating resonance similar to the way one would vibrate a tuning fork. This vibrating did not affect the propulsion of the craft, but simply duplicated in a precise manner the same type of vibrations produced in the fault lines. If they had not taken this precaution they would have been affected by the frequency barrier as man had been."

"Documented accounts reveal that the wild animals and those in zoos become restless just before impending changes such as earthquakes, which indicates that they are aware of changes in the frequency barrier. According to psychiatrists, mentally disturbed individuals, even though in a darkened room unable to see the moon, will react to the various stages of the moon. This is because the magnetic field that surrounds the planet also encompasses the orbit of the moon. The magnetic field of Earth is associated strongly with the electromagnetic frequency barrier, so as the moon moves into various areas of the magnetic field of the planet, it would affect the frequency barrier. The frequency barrier, in turn, affects the bio-electromagnetic thinking processes of the brain of man, and the mentally ill are affected to a greater degree."

"In the present transitional period approaching the New Age, the frequency barrier has lessened and will eventually, in that New Age, disappear forever. We are progressing, not

Fig. 1. Neanderthal Man

Fig. 2. Java Man

Fig. 3. Cro-Magnon Man

Fig. 4. Egyptian Man

regressing. We are returning to the unrestricted mental state, as it was before the great deluge. Man of Earth today is looking to the heavens for new knowledge to fill the newly-awakened parts of his mind. Based upon scientific studies of the frequency barrier's decrease throughout history, some have proposed its total removal by the last half of this decade."

• • •

5. As interest in this subject deepened and I researched other materials, it became clear that the Guardians of our planet related Earth's frequency barrier to the fall of Maldek. Maldek was the fifth planet from our sun and existed for eons of time with a greater civilization than our own, which finally destroyed itself through a nuclear war out of control and slow-falling radiation dust which brought madness and loss of all reason to the planetary population, followed by a total annihilation of their world. It is the motivation, and not the details which led to its destruction, that is important here. Maldek was destroyed through its own refusal to become a part of the Galactic Pact for Universal Peace and its own pride, which refused the cooperation and unity of any other planets or the Confederation, thereby nullifying any acts of assistance or intervention, under Galactic Law.

For a certain cycle of time our solar system passed through a mass of cosmic debris and radiation dust of Maldek residue, effecting physical and mental changes and behavioral madness in Eartheans. No other planets were affected; only the Earth did not have the substance within its atmosphere and soil to counteract this action. This unfortunate path has been traversed and is behind us, alleviated greatly by the cleansing actions of the Guardian fleets.

6. However, the cosmic mystery still pressed for further solution when it was discovered that radiations from our own sun were harmful to Earth's inhabitants when allowed to penetrate through the ionosphere layer. The Guardians found that

the radiations not only accented adverse attitudes, but actually produced a hindrance to the *beneficial* cosmic rays beamed to the planet.

Our cosmic history of spiritual retardation made Earth-eans unique in their destructive inner competitiveness and combativeness amongst each other. The consciousness-stunting poisonous rays from our physical sun are now being screened off by counter radiation effects generated by our Space Friends. Eight hundred and sixty-four miles beyond our planet's circumference is the Earth's ionosphere, which any missile can penetrate and puncture in less than ten minutes. We are warned by those who guard us that rifts in that ionosphere caused by nuclear tests results in the seepage of destruction into our planet's atmosphere.

At this point in my thinking I deliberately sought and obtained an audience with science technician, Soltec, Commander of the Space Monitoring craft, the "Phoenix," who answered many questions and contributed a message for this chapter:

1. "I am Soltec, representing the Brothers of Light, both in the Hierarchal body of this solar system and the Intergalactic Council who guard the planet Earth. As astrophysicist and continual science monitor for our Council, I do attest to the presence over billions of years of an interrupting factor in the atmosphere of Earth which, down through eons of time, has been an inhibiting factor in the developing awareness of humanity upon the planet.

7. "The frequency barrier is related to two factors—one being the dust of Maldek, as it was almost permanently impregnated into Earth's atmosphere following that heart-breaking catastrophe. The second factor is adverse radiation produced by your own sun.

"Long ago there came to our attention the great difference that existed surrounding and upon Earth as compared with all other planets of the universe. We discovered, in our continual observation of your world, that a negative influence penetrated your atmosphere, producing conditions that existed nowhere else in space. We saw the results of this as souls were placed and seeded upon the planet; their genes would undergo changes, and interference which was present in the offspring was unlike the genes of the parents who bore them—parents who had, themselves, come from other worlds. Long centuries of observation indicated that something peculiar to Earth alone was preventing its expansion on spiritual levels, a factor that did not exist elsewhere. We began extensive scientific pursuit of this mystery to determine and remove the problem humanity faced.

8. "In our floating laboratory, a craft called the Phoenix, we have explored and pursued this problem diligently. It was a great source of joy to all of us when we determined the factor of the harmfulness of your sun's rays, which were seeping through your weakened ionosphere in a harmful way. The action of these rays has now been counterbalanced considerably over a long gradual period of time. We have introduced other rays into your atmosphere which now, in your day, enable you of Earth to return to your own original human magnetic force-field of Light, *enabling your spiritual awareness* to flourish as it was intended.

"The radiations you have endured resulting from the destruction of Maldek are held at bay through our mending of the abrasions and rifts occurring in the ionosphere belt which surrounds the planet. The work of the thousands of fleets of volunteer craft circling the globe have labored long and lovingly upon this problem.

5. "The debris of Maldek carries destructive elements, reminiscent of their former errors in evolution—when they permitted themselves to be partakers of mental deterioration through their careless ventures into nuclear technology. Their deeds of research and war permitted the dust of destruction to destroy their planetary safety belt, deranging the minds of their

population through indiscriminate exposure to the resulting radiation. They turned deaf ears to the pleas of the Council for peace and refused any offers of help. This prevented any intervention on our part because of the policies set by the Intergalactic Council on Non-Intervention. Thus, through the will of the determined inhabitants, a beautiful star was lost from the firmament and its contaminating dust released to float in the atmosphere of Earth and Mars, where depressions and craters resulted. Rings of debris were formed around Saturn, and the unwholesome fall of destructive particles settled in the atmosphere surrounding Earth. It still remains; we cannot remove it, but we do continually labor to preserve your ionosphere as a protective layer, not only from the radiation residue, but from the rays of your sun.

"The counteracting rays now shining upon you have once again brought mankind an opportunity for spiritual quest and the awakening of his inherent spiritual powers not possible when the frequency barrier was affecting men's minds.

5. "Once again, Man of the outer universe can come to you and touch your lives with our nearness and our help to you. If you permit yourselves to indulge in thermonuclear destruction, your planet will be lost when its protective layer disintegrates. This is the hour when humanity must count the cost and not deafen their ears to the call, as did Maldek. We encourage humanity to rise in its frequency while that is still possible, so that millions of your inhabitants will invite our assistance which will permit our intervention in your destruction. If enough of mankind calls in concern for your world, we can come and prevent your total annihilation. Maldek did not have those who would call; those who would reach for divine intervention; and so, the results of that choice now film the outer rim of your own world. We plead with Eartheans to join in the call that will bring us to you with awareness and delivery from disaster that will destroy you should our invitation remain unheeded.

9. "Work for disarmament and strive for Peace on Earth, that your beautiful planet may remain to enjoy its destiny. The barrier that once would have prevented your call has now been brought under control *unless* you resort to nuclear war. Your tests and underground explosions have set the Earth to boiling within; your upper land tests have already torn holes in your upper atmosphere that only we can repair. You are on the brink of a Maldek destiny unless you respond in a sane manner to my words.

"Now is the time to accept the call of this book and raise your spiritual attainment to its highest level, that our vibrations might blend with your own to save your world. If you call, we will answer. I am Soltec, who speaks in the Name of Our Radiant One."

• • •

Commander Hatonn, of our galaxy, has also released a statement for this chapter:

"Every day that passes, the fog of effluvia that hangs over the Earth is penetrated by the new effects from the Great Central Sun and the winds of change that envelop your world. We who watch have our instruments constantly tuned in to the vibrational patterns of the planet and its people. I would like to address myself to the change of frequency barrier that has very slowly taken place, for your sakes.

"It has taken many civilizations for the effects of any change to gradually work out evidential facts of improvement. One looks in retrospect over the slow manifestation of progress, so-called, in the life of humanity. All major changes and improvements through science, enlightenment, religion, health and medicine, are the result of the lessening frequency barrier. Inspired men in tune with Infinite Intelligence have thus brought to mankind the giant steps of progress for the life of humanity on Earth. The gradual shifting of the veils of the mysteries of life have also been evidential of this gradual change. Each decade has brought a loosening of old crystalliza-tions of thought, so that new thought or new understanding could take place.

"As preponderances of Light have infiltrated human soci-ety, beings of other dimensions have been enabled to place thoughts of the highest nature through those waiting in-telligences who seek information from the highest Source. We must therefore lend assurance to that position which does declare that ongoing Light is accomplishing greater things. The malignant forces of war and destruction do actively exist and carry on their side of a divine program, but the forces of Divine Light have made incontestable advances into the ramparts of ignorance throughout the last decade.

"We now combine our efforts to weaken bigotry and ridicule that have divided man from his birthright of cosmic communication. There is no limitation other than that which is self-created. Our entire Confederation does now record the softest call of our name and stand ready to respond."

• • •

I must confess that I was rather amazed at the inrush of the great wise ones who desired to be heard when I was absorbed with the study of the frequency barrier. Master Her-mes came with these words:

11. "We of the Celestial Kingdom have long struggled with the problem of the frequency barrier around planet Earth. It exists nowhere else and is the source of that term which calls Earth the 'dark planet.' Other worlds have had to overcome many obstacles, but none have had to cope with this particular problem in their struggles toward spiritual progress. The dark barrier is composed of hindering frequencies which took their greatest toll in the mental body of your inhabitants.

"In spite of the dark circle which has engulfed Earth's sphere, many great ones and aspired ones, highborn from ethe-ria, have entered this barrier in a sacrificial effort to assist in its

59

disintegration by bringing infusions of Light from their own Being. The ring of darkness *does not have its effect on these who thus come on missions of mercy* to Terra.

"It is from this framework of volunteer force that the great changes and uplifting of life upon the planet has been wrought. At times it has seemed that the progress was infinitesimal, yet nevertheless, one can appreciate the great strides onward in the restoration of a once beautiful planet.

"Millions of souls have arisen beyond the barrier and participated in the program of Light in spite of it, and this has held the planet steady and intact. This progressive assault against the frequency barrier of Earth has all but reduced its effects to the self-determined few who choose not to see the way. But they shall not restore the darkness that once engulfed the earth, for its destiny now is assured. The cleansing of its frequencies and magnetic field will return this world to the edenic beauty and peace once known here.

"Now, at this time, all inhabitants are limited in only their own desires to become Man in his highest form of manifestation—as Sons of God."

"I am Hermes who speaks, the Father of Wisdom."

• • •

We close our discussion of the frequency barrier with these words received from our beloved Jesus-Sananda:

"Many have sought a simple way to write of the restoration of humanity to that original state when they literally spoke with the gods. This was the natural order of things until the veil fell across the minds of men.

12. "This has been called by some a frequency barrier; others have termed it the 'fall of man'." It has been touched upon in various terminologies, but its effect was ever the same—the lie of separation penetrated the human force-field with the increase of physical density, and the barrier of incompatibility became the norm of man's life upon this planet.

"Therefore the gods themselves have walked the earth again and again down through the corridors of time, to erase the fallacy of man's separation from his own indwelling divinity. As this barrier of error has been lessened through unfolding wisdom, the created has found his voice to speak with his Creator once again."

• • •

So you see, my friends, at our point in time on the very threshold of our Golden Age, with all barriers lifted and hindrances removed, if we do not pursue the spiritual quest now...we are without excuse!

Think on These Things

1. What is the "frequency barrier"?
2. How long did it last?
3. How did it affect humanity?
4. How did the extraterrestrials adapt their craft to the earth's frequency barrier?
5. What led to the fall of Maldek?
6. Name some harmful effects of solar radiation discovered by Space Brothers' research?
7. What factors produced the frequency barrier?
8. How did the Guardians solve the solar rays problem?
9. How can the planet Earth avoid the fate of Maldek?
10. How did the lessening of the frequency barrier affect world progress?
11. How did the Spiritual Hierarchy deal with the effects of the frequency barrier?
12. Define the "veil that fell across the minds of men."

NOTES:

V
The Dynamics of Frequency

It is important that a clear-cut distinction be made in our understanding of the difference between *mind* and *brain*. Monka, of the Great Cosmic Tribunal, has sent a message for you which is not only beautiful, but contributes much to our understanding this distinction:

"We are sending this book to mankind with the benediction of the Brotherhood of Light, and the Presence of Greater Light with all who seek to know the truth. It is written that only as one becomes as the little child shall one enter the portals of wisdom.

1. & 2. "The Mind is a fragment of Universal Allness. It is associated in the thinking of humanity with the human brain. Actually the Mind is related to the physical brain as its avenue of expression, its channel of flow and its contact with the physical octave. Mind is eternal. It is that fragment of creation which returns again and again, the uniqueness of what you call Soul, which clothes itself with many different physical brains as that ongoing 'soul' expands its experiences as manifested fragments of the Universal Creator.

3. "Thus *Mind is the avenue of the Cosmos into a human lifestream.* Man must realize that the tie of his own being to the Omniverse is through the flow of Mind into his physical being.

63

Therefore, it is through the attachment of Mind to the tensor sector of the brain that the flow of Universal Thought comes to one in embodiment. Here we find the eternal flow of all wisdom, all knowledge, all understanding, without limitation. All of these things are outside of man himself. They flow as a river into the tensor area, there to be placed in the pathway of the cortex and claimed for rightful use. This is the avenue of inspiration, the threshold of genius, and the total source of all inventiveness and creativity. Here are the poet's words, the music of the song, the beauty and the vision of the artist, the ingenuity of the great discoveries and unfoldment of the progress of humanity.

"Many thousands of words could be written on this fact, but most would be misunderstood until the soul-mind center is awakened to its proper place in the evolvement of the race toward its true identity as Man in the Cosmos.

4. "I am one who has participated in the program of Light for this planet through century after century, eons after eons of time. How beautiful it has been to behold the awakening of the human thought world to the flow of Divinity through the spiritual Mind and to see the glorification of that life as it becomes integrated with its spiritual purpose and mission. The purpose, the direction, the mission will all flow in revelation to that soul who has learned to *set aside the logical and reasoning faculties*, to clear the path for the inspirational flow.

"With Divine integration of soul and body, through spirit, or love—it is then and only then that human becomes true Man and a functioning, productive cell in the universal body of the cosmos."

• • •

5. In the early sixties, Gabriel Green, Editor of *U.F.O. International Magazine*, carried an outstanding series of articles containing the experiences and transmissions received by Bob Renaud, through an electronics set-up of various forms of

equipment in his basement. Bob spoke with the same group of Space Friends over a long period of time in a two-way conversation by radio means, and viewed them inside their craft on his specially adapted T.V. screen. A lengthy quote from this material is presented here, a passage discussing telepathy.

"The ultraconscious is the sixth sense, and the vehicle for parapsychic functions such as telepathy, clairaudience, clairvoyance, etc.

"The unifier, or unifying level, is the highest state, the level at which all matter in the Universe is in rapport with the combined All-Mind, known by other names, among them Almighty, Creator, and God.

"This level is the one in which every existent thing is united with every other. All minds are as one, and the energies forming matter are a part of it likewise. The All-Mind controls the Universe to the limits possible. It does not know the future, and cannot cause predestination. While each person is part of the All-Mind, the conscious is the personality and individuality, and is not controlled by the All-Mind to the extent of interference in the conscious mind's affairs.

"One level that we are to discuss in particular is the ultraconscious. It is controlled directly by both the conscious and the All-Mind, and is the conscious' direct link with the Universe, matter and energy. This level is the seat of all psychic abilities.

"First, telepathy. In simple terms, it is mind-to-mind resonance. The mind is a form of energy with a set frequency, different from any other. While this frequency cannot be changed, there is another, a universal frequency, which can be turned on or off at will by the individual. It is on this frequency that telepathy occurs.

"When the mind is not generating this frequency, it will neither transmit nor receive impulses, and will be impervious to telepathy. When generated, however, it is receptive to messages from throughout the Universe. It can select from any of these at will, shutting out all others. When this is done, then an automatic psychic block is imposed that forbids listening in by others not involved.

"This rapport can be established between any number of minds, but once set, it is impervious to outside probing, by either psychic or electronic means.

"Usually, no one keeps his mind open to calls, and so a form of mental paging is used to gain the desired party's attention. Then, by telepathy, the communication can begin.

"The people who have developed their telepathic abilities can change the phasing of their transceptor frequency at will, which is usually necessary, since the impulses are almost never synchronized to the extent required.

"You of Earth are unfortunately too close-minded about telepathy and related phenomena to bother developing your latent abilities. Once you arrive at an age of five years or more, it is extremely difficult to stimulate the growth of telepathy. It must be cultivated from birth."

We are all aware of the tremendous advancement of the technology of other worlds compared to our own. Another passage in the Renaud material is fascinating, as the Space Friends reveal the method that is used when it is time for a new breakthrough to be presented to the earth, and clearly imply that our global inventors and great scientists and humanitarians receive their inspirational ideas through the use of outer space technology, the technology of mind impression:

6. "The operation to which we refer is called the Somnivision Project. With it ideas are imprinted into selected people during sleep, which these subjects then credit to themselves.

"In principle, the human mind is a form of energy. When in the body, each mind has a distinct frequency of operation, depending on the particular characteristics of that brain which it inhabits. While we do not completely understand it, we know that it has to do with magnetic or, as you call it, electrical, circuit dimensions within the neurons.

"The instrument used to produce Somnivision, the Omni-frequency Psychprint Unit, is designed to register this characteristic frequency via a probe beam, which is trained on the mind from a unit in a small, three-foot diameter scout ship.

6. "Whenever Somnivision is to be undertaken, a beam is set up from a scout hovering low over the home of the person to be impressed, and a relay is begun through it to the mind. Since the frequencies are phased, any modulation on the beam would be considered by the brain as an impulse from the mind itself, and treated as another thought.

"Depending on the strength of this beam, we can cause anything from merely a vague memory of the 'dream' to a verbatim recording in the brain.

"This can be compared to a radio feeding a tape recorder. When the incoming signal is weak and distorted, only occasional snatches of the program are intelligible. As the signal strength increases, more is recorded that can be understood, until, at a high strength, the tape is an exact duplicate of the program.

"The great inventions of your time—radio, television, nuclear power, and the airplane, for example—are for the most part a result of this imprinting.

"The reason we do this during sleeping hours is that we find that in a conscious state, the active mind tends to distort the information according to its own experiences, prejudices, and theories, rather than taking it as is. To prevent this, we choose a time when both the conscious and subconscious mind can be by-passed. Sleep is that time."

"In certain instances, we use infraception, a variation of Somnivision, which imprints on a level of consciousness just below the conscious. This you call 'daydreaming.'"

While the processes described are not directly associated with telepathy, they do show the action of the Higher Mind in receiving the "imprint" and holding it for conscious mind (or cortexial action) to discover later. I have checked this informa-

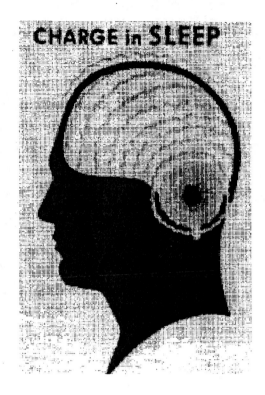

tion with Space Friends who contact me, and found that most of the groups do use this or similar technology when works of highest nature, including keeping the peace, are beamed to the planet.

• • •

7. Having given some consideration to the distinction between Mind and brain, we also need to make a distinction between thinking and thought. Universal Mind, or the mental continuum, interpenetrates all dimensions and therefore, knows no limitations to hinder the flow of thought. The physical brain is subject to limitation of the ability of one to think, but thinking is not the act of Mind; it is the activity of the cortex surrounding the outer edge of the brain.

8. & 9. Thought occurs within Mind, which is your Higher Christ Self—the uniqueness that is you. It is aware of all that is happening to you and all of your thinking processes. Anything and everything in our entire Universe and every dimension it encompasses can be penetrated by thought, which

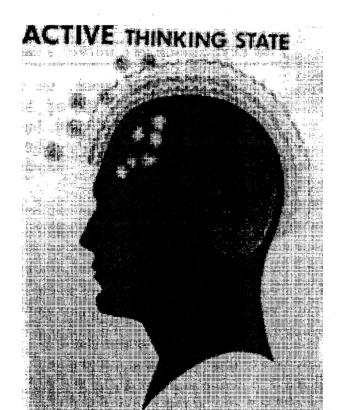

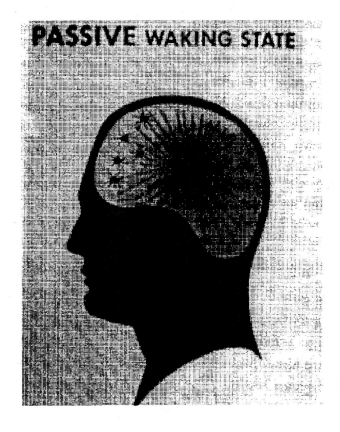

is the Christ action within you. We have stressed over and over that telepathy is Mind-to-Mind contact. It is Mind action before it is deposited into the brain thinking processes. Thought enters the tensor sector of the brain from Mind, or Christ Self. Basically, then, telepathy is communication between your higher self and the higher self of another living being. One places a thought within the other, or sends a thought to the other, where it is held in store for the thinking brain, which in turn converts the thought into something it can recognize or understand

7.–11. Keep ever before you the fact that your Mind is a spiritual part of you outside of your physical form and therefore, outside of your brain. Brain indulges in thinking; Mind brings in thought. As your ability to work with Higher Mind develops, your eager Mind, piercing the heights of mental awareness, will lead you into the higher thought emanations from great Teachers in the outer Universe. They anxiously await the flight of your receptive Mind—or Soulself—into their dimensions of great Truth, for they are only a thought away. Telepathy is passive perception; suddenly the thought-idea is simply there, and you *perceive* its presence. A nontelepath only receives through the physical senses.

Recently, following a message from Commander Anton, I asked a technical question on just what was taking place in our communication process. His reply was so simple:

"The words you are receiving are being induced into your brain through your own energy field as I project my energies toward you. Our communication is mind to mind, and not with a beam."

In the earliest years of my own efforts in this direction, when I knew nothing of such terms as frequencies, energies, and magnetic fields, and the whole array of terms we are now so accustomed to, I received an interesting explanation of the process in my higher contacts at the time. One of my group of Teachers who had me in tow during that period, called Apollo, released this discourse in 1970:

"Your ability to sense or feel our messages is entirely a frequency phenomenon. We are attuned to your ability to receive, just as any receiving mechanism might be, as you are also attuned to us. The human forcefield, or aura, is a magneto of currents pulling into its center from the energies that surround it. At the same time it is also sending outward its own energies into the atmosphere again. This is pulsating life! This is Oneness with the Universe and this is that which evolves on and on, in everlasting motion in everlasting space (*Resonance!*). This nucleus of energy current is that influence one feels, which brings pleasure or pain upon association.

"The higher frequency souls appear different, respond differently and bring a different change in the atmosphere they displace. Yes, displacement takes place, but not as you interpret the idea. There is a constant, repeated cycle of in and outward streaks of power (*Synaptic action!*) from the soul center (*tensor area*) which are constantly recharged and returned.

12. "Each organ of the physical body has, in turn, its own magnetic field of various frequencies, and all flow together to produce the whole in this electrical-like aura, which is the soul. We bring to mind the blazing electrical advertising signs in your cities. In their display, each individual bulb is placed at various frequencies in an on and off sequence, and together produce the whole in a coordinated result, presenting a message or a moving picture to the eye. You are aware only of the apparent picture, and not what made it so. Similarly, each various organ of the body contributes to the frequency pattern of the whole, each dependent upon the energy—the peculiar frequency—of the other to coordinate the uniqueness of your personal frequency to which we attune. This is the principle behind the statement that 'illness is only a maladjustment in body frequencies, short-circuiting the whole.'"

• • •

Orthon, Adamski's space contact, teacher and friend, summed it all with his brief definition: "Mental telepathy is a unified state of consciousness between two points—the sender and the receiver—and distance is no barrier whatsoever."

Think on These Things

1. Can you differentiate between Mind and Brain?
2. What is the relationship of mind to soul?
3. Explain the "avenue of inspiration."
4. What is meant by spiritual integration?
5. Who was Bob Renaud?
6. What is Somnivision?
7. What is thinking?
8. What is thought?
9. What is telepathy?
10. Where is Mind?
11. How does a non-telepath receive information?
12. What is the human aura?

NOTES:

VII
The Dynamics of
The Human Brain

1. As we consider all of the facets of cosmic telepathy, it will be worthwhile to spend a portion of time examining that marvelously designed creation—the human brain. It is an outstanding computer, and its original model still works just fine. It is a memory bank, an up-to-date communications system, a generator for the body plant, a dynamometer, a chemical laboratory, a picture tube, and an antenna to heaven. It is a coordinator of our spiritual, mental, emotional and physical systems as it signals from inner space all that touches our entire being and world!

2. There are four primary forces in Universe, two of which we desire to touch upon here. These forces make up the one power that runs all of the Cosmos, sustains life and all intelligence. One is sometimes called Spirit, sometimes called Resonating Electromagnetic Force; the other we know as electricity. It is present in our personal vibration and our mind propulsion. Science is aware of the last, but does not understand the first. Electricity is an expression of physical energy, and physical energy is associated with the physical brain. Spirit is an expression of mental energy, and mental energy is associated with mind—Universal Mind.

3. Science can record and measure electrical currents in

the brain. They know that mental and emotional disturbances create electrical storms in the brain when consciousness is excited. They know that intense emotions can generate more energy and project stronger thought. Metaphysicians are well versed in the Universal law that states, "Energy follows thought." Nerve impulses in the brain are both electrical and chemical processes. Sodium and potassium electrically charge the atoms that send the impulses. We have an old saying, "When the spirit moves me, I'll do it," especially when the lady of the house approaches her spouse to fix the back porch or paint the kitchen, because it is her thought and not his. But if he wakes some morning and the thought has been placed in the pathway of consciousness, "I ought to paint that kitchen today," then energy will follow that thought, atoms send the impulses, and desire and action follow. One Space Brother explained it this way: "Our living cells of energy contain light waves which send out electrical waves, which form into thought. We accomplish things in this way, for all thoughts are things to come." We have another wonderful Universal Law: "We create our own pathway by the way we think!" So it is and so be it. Do not crumble or whine or complain about your lot in life or flounder in morbid self-pity. *YOU DO NOT LIKE YOUR LIFE...CHANGE IT!*

2. However, let us clearly define another principle. Electrical impulses are subservient to spiritual law—Universal Law. Brain is less than mind, and so it is that we all recall the adage, "Mind over matter."

Now that science has begun to shed light through investigation of the mind and the electrical impulses of the brain, what was once considered spooky is now seen to be a natural phenomenon and the right of man on earth by Divine Unction. Nothing in the physical Universe can escape the penetration of a thought, including the farthest galaxy.

In the following pages there will appear several sketches of a medial sagittal section of the brain, but rather than have to repeat such a mouthful twice, shall we just call this fellow "George"? "George" will help us to understand where the various key parts of the brain are located while we attempt to share a layman's conception of the function of these various parts.

As we consult with George, our attention is drawn first to the Master glands—the pineal and the pituitary (refer to illustration, page 77). The pituitary is located behind the eye level and has been called the body receiving set. As a thought receiver it is your contact point within the physical brain that enables the thought of another positive point (sender) to be placed in the resonating tensor center of your brain for further interpretation. It is an interesting fact that the autopsy on George Adamski showed an extremely over-developed pituitary gland. The pituitary acts as a toggle switch; "on" as the will, when sending; "off" as passive, when receiving.

5. The pineal, which is the true Master gland, is the thought transmitter and is a positive terminal. Sometimes it is called the "third eye" because of its nature and position in line with the middle forehead, and when this gland has fully opened in spiritual awareness, those with eyes to see perceive the ray of Golden Cosmic Light coming forth from the forehead area as a star. We read of this seal in the forehead in the Book of Revelation, a seal placed by the angels of God and a mark of protection. In describing the symbol of the Knights of the Solar Cross, George Hunt Williamson explained that there was an eye on the shield because these sons and daughters of God have a highly developed pineal gland, a third eye, which gives them outstanding telepathic abilities. He claimed the Knights of the Solar Cross examine men with this "eye" rather than just normal vision, which would allow only for reason and logic instead of truth and understanding.

Cosmic Master Aljanon, a representative of both the Brotherhood and the Confederation, has given us two interesting paragraphs:

YOUR PERSONAL COMMUNICATIONS SYSTEM

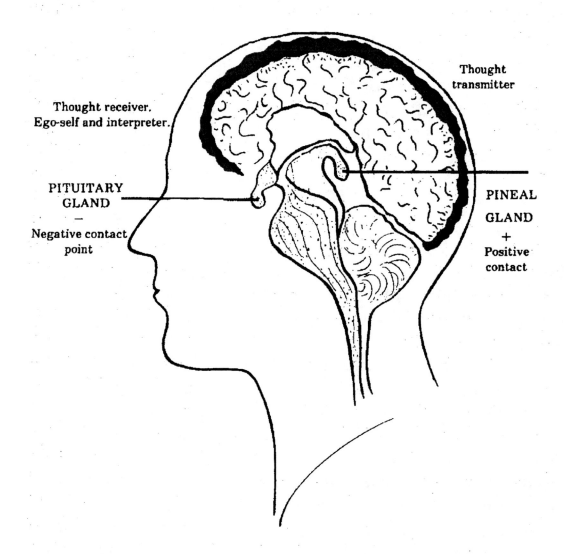

Thought transmitter

Thought receiver. Ego-self and interpreter.

PITUITARY GLAND — Negative contact point

PINEAL GLAND + Positive contact

"Science speaks of inversion or repulsion as an opposing force. So it is that there is a negative and a positive force ever pulsating through the channels of Mind in the inflow and out-flow of atoms of energy and their reaction upon the human brain cells. Positive action flows through the pineal doorway, while negative action flows through the pituitary doorway, both reacting in unison in the balancing of all the activity of the mental faculties."

"As the world stands waiting to learn of telepathic abilities, the glands of the human form will be injected with powerful rays and influence from outer space which will expand the abilities of the pituitary and pineal glands, awakening their capabilities gradually, throughout society. In many cases this will have an adverse reaction and perverted use, yet in a large number of the population this will be a positive thing. The times have not permitted this before now, but now many converging facts are preparing humanity for a broad scope of spiritual awareness to penetrate planetary life."

• • •

6. Once again, consulting with our friend George, notice the heavily darkened strip surrounding the brain just under the skullcap (refer to illustration on page 79). This is the cerebral cortex, or simpler still, the cortex, and that is where all of the action is. It is a sinuous, ridged, winding, surface layer about ¼ inch thick, like a grey grapefruit rind. It curves around the skull area of the brain surrounding both hemispheres of the cerebrum. It represents about ⅕, or 20%, of the brain weight.

7. This is the area where thinking, logic, reason, deduction, evaluation, classifying, short-term memory takes place. Here is the control of the functions of the five physical senses, and the movement of all of the extremities. It can guess, calculate, assimilate. Like a firehose, it pours a constant barrage into the subconscious, of your experiences and the feelings they aroused. It receives only through the senses, and is the information gatherer for the whole brain and various levels of consciousness.

Since this cortex is the location of all thinking and reasoning, it therefore creates mental interference or static *that constantly interferes with any telepathic function.* The normal consciously awake state is comprised of cortical activity. Consequently, if we are going to awaken the sleeping giant in our spiritual resonating tensor sector (more later on this), then we

THE CORTICAL FUNCTIONS OF THE BRAIN
CONSCIOUS CONSCIOUSNESS

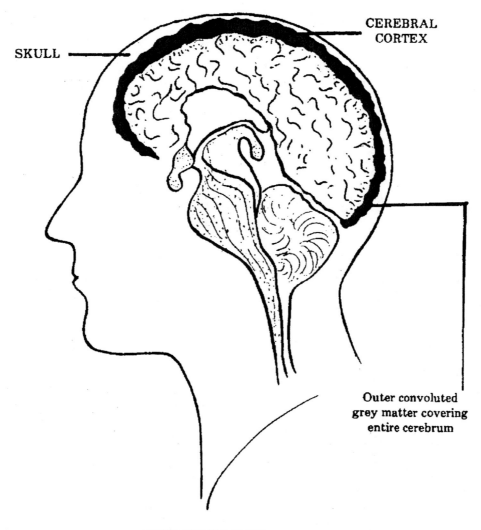

SKULL

CEREBRAL
CORTEX

Outer convoluted
grey matter covering
entire cerebrum

YOUR THINK TANK

must create a pause or stillness in the busy beehive-like cortex in order that spiritual or Universal impulses, or implanted thoughts, can get through the *jammed switchboard.* Following that, the information can be passed along to the cortical or conscious center.

Have you ever been walking down a path and looked

down and discovered something there? Likewise, if the busy thinking cortex is not too narrowly focused on a subject, it will come across a thought in its path and assimilate it into its general content and initiate action. Think of a resting of the cortex as a "pause that refreshes" the mind. How many many times all of us have found a moment of reverie, perhaps in sitting looking at a lake or a beautiful snowfall, or hulling peas on the back porch, or meditatively even doing an ironing, and suddenly realize..."a thought came to me." Or perhaps just a quick drop into a favorite easy chair in a pause from activity, and when quiet, "...suddenly I knew what to do" about this or that problem. Awakening early in the morning, refreshed from rest and in that short pause before the busy consciousness gets back into control, many wonderful thoughts from Universal Mind will be discovered and you will be impressed to do thus and so. This is because concentration or active thinking is the function of the cortical section of the brain. When it is racing full speed ahead trying to think through a solution, it is not a conducive condition toward capturing or recognizing a message from the spiritual tensor center. On the contrary, reasoning and deep thought obstruct our ability to function telepathically. How many times well-meaning friends might say to you, "Well, sleep on it and it won't look so bad in the morning." This is technically a true statement. After giving the cortex a "break," or by the dawn's early light, something of value has been placed in the pathway of the cortex that brings comfort, relief and solution because it has come from Universal Mind, and the Heavenly Father. So friends, sleep on it—and wake up with an answer! If these momentary, or spontaneous, pauses can bring a measure of results, then how much more positive and fulfilling to the soul and guidance for life's pathway will be the deliberate solitude and the premeditated stillness spent in practicing the Presence of the Father in the motionlessness of communion with Him and hearing the still small voice from deep within. Try it...you'll like it!

● ● ●

9. As you locate the cerebellum in the sketch of George (refer to illustration on page 82), you will see it is located at the base of the curve of the head. The cerebellum is a kind of "half-way house" to the unconscious. It functions as a storage house until its accumulated information is finally taken to the unconscious basement. It also will bring up information from there when conscious cortex demands it. It also measures our mental coordination on how well the cortical department communicates with the subconscious.

It also automatically regulates the vital functions of the body and the habit patterns. Its action with the vital functions can be interfered with through abnormal fears, worries, hates, destructive emotions. This explains psychosomatic illnesses, in which perfectly well organs seem to fail in their functions for no explainable physical cause. The cerebellum also coordinates muscle action with body equilibrium, controlling balance and posture and keeping us from falling flat on our face when we decide to stand, as it enters the brainstem and goes down the spine. It is a good friend, and takes care of us in many ways.

● ● ●

10. The thalamus is a mass of ganglionic nuclei radiating to almost every portion of the cortex just as various parts of the cerebral cortex relay streams of fibers to the thalamus (refer to illustration on page 83). Its grey matter mass is divided by a vertical strip of white matter which we will discuss presently. The spontaneous electrical activity of the busy cerebral cortex is stimulated from the thalamus, which sustains and regulates the normal resting rhythms of the cortex. This information I found to be most interesting in view of the "thalamatic pause" as taught by Soltec through spiritual messenger Richard Miller, as a necessary requirement in achieving higher level tensor activity in meditation.

The thalamus is the highest segment of the brainstem of

YOUR MENTAL BASEMENT AND SUBCONSCIOUS STOREHOUSE
THE CEREBELLUM

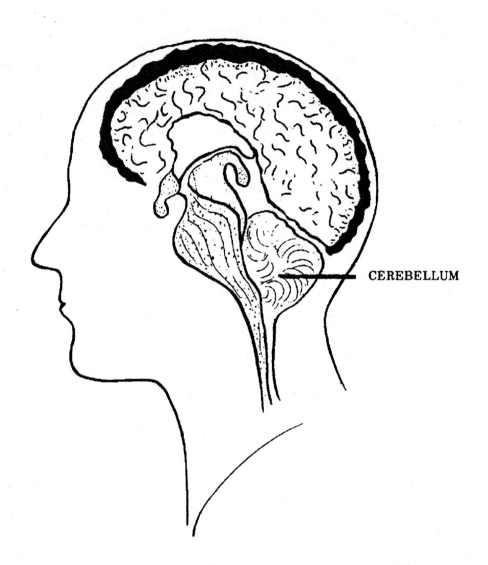

CEREBELLUM

which the inner core is made up of white matter. There are two thalami—one in the right brain hemisphere and one in the left. This is where dreams are formed. This area is also a memory bank. It has nerves especially designed for forming mental images. When the thalamus is energized during sleep we have dreams in either black and white or color. The thalamus is our mental television.

It is an electromagnetic area that reacts immediately to

YOUR MENTAL TELEVISION

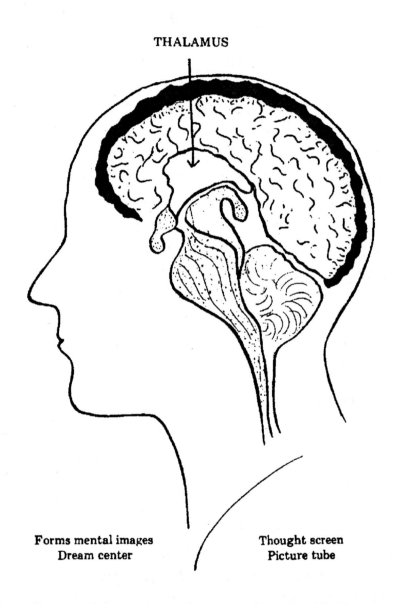

THALAMUS

Forms mental images
Dream center

Thought screen
Picture tube

strong emotion, fears, and sets up a building blueprint. If you are thinking right, it will attract to you conditions, circumstances, resources, even people you need to meet to bring you your desires.

Remember these facts: The thalamus is the seat of emotion, and the busy cortex is the seat of discrimination. When

83

they are integrated and balanced in a warm relationship, the emotions are made richer and relaxed by association with the cortex. As Soltec has said through channel Richard Miller: "Thinking and *feeling*—not just feeling—that is the thalamatic pause." Continuing the statement of Cosmic Master Aljanon quoted earlier, he stated further:

11. "Mind is most like the equipment of the scientist when it is placing pictures upon the screen of the thalamus in exactly the same manner as your television technique places a picture in your living room. The mind has its screen for receiving its projection, just as you have yours in a box. The audio and the video are both present in the brain in all the identical parts and actions that are present in modern broadcast technology. The human body is the pattern for all discovery or true invention. It reveals the secrets of discovery to the eager waiting searcher for methods and means."

• • •

The synapses nerve ends reach up from the resonating cerebrum and come near, but do not touch the nerve ends dangling from the cortex. (refer to illustration on page 85). The "nerve message" is conveyed to the cortex by a tiny electrical spark, perhaps similar to spark plug action in a vehicle.

Those that are active are heavy and dark, developed and functioning most of the time. The majority, however, are pale grey and not in use and not fully developed.

The term "tensor" is a phrase coined to define the potential for thought depth that exists in your synapses area, that one might consider the means whereby new synaptical junctions may be opened to the *idle and unused portion of the brain.*

As we employ the techniques of stilling the cortex *we are opening up new synapses as awareness transforms the mental process.* New impulse channels from nerve cell to nerve cell are opened which have never been used before. These signals from inner space are evidence of spiritual awakening.

SIGNALS FROM INNER SPACE
THE SYNAPSES

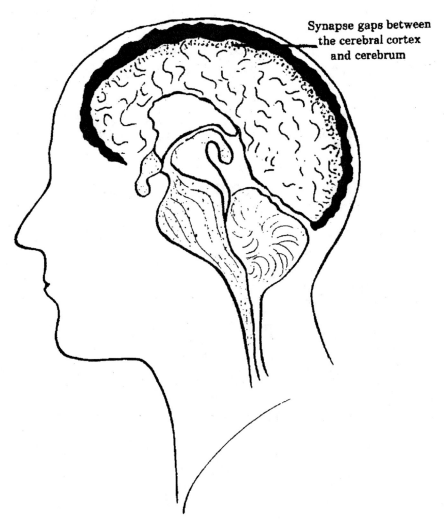

Synapse gaps between
the cerebral cortex
and cerebrum

Synaptic Transmission
Individual nerve cells are in close contact at
synapses, where functional connections occur.

Think on These Things

1. Describe some of the functions of the human brain.
2. What is the difference between electricity and Spirit?
3. Explain the principle, "Energy follows thought."
4. Distinguish between the pineal and the pituitary glands, in location and function.
5. What is the "seal in the forehead" described in the Book of Revelation?
6. Describe and locate the cerebral cortex.
7. What is the physical function of the cortex?
8. Why does it interfere with telepathy?
9. Why is the cerebellum called a "half-way house" and where is it located?
10. What is the relationship of the thalamus to the cortex, and why is the thalamatic pause necessary to telepathic endeavor?
11. Why is the thalamus similar to modern broadcasting technology?
12. What sand where are the synaptical junctions and how do they relate to spiritual awareness?

NOTES:

VIII
The Dynamics
Tensor Power

The term "tensor" was first used by Wilbert B. Smith in 1951. He was a radio and electrical engineer who received the term through telepathic communication with our Space Friends. It was used as another name for the caduceus coil which could be used to awaken the dormant section of the brain. Mr. Smith actually built a tensor coil and had it patented.

Commander Hatonn, of our galaxy, refers to this dormant area of the brain in this brief message:

"'All is mind' is given as the first of the seven great principles. Each section of the human consciousness is important. Each division has its role to play in total awareness. Humanity is not using all of its capacity. When the unused portion of the brain is awakened and activated, the entire life and the four lower bodies will enter a change. All phases of that manifestation will be accelerated, clarified and brightened."

1. "Therefore, this quest is not merely an effort in communication or to master cosmic telepathy. Telepathy is but an arm of a greater thing you have termed total awareness. It is to find a total attunement with the Infinite One from the soul level of Being, responding and vibrating with Universal Mind and the Creator.

"So consider these things. Consider the vehicle that moves along the highway operating on only one-fifth of its cylinder power, and be not like that vehicle, but travel through life in your full capacity and you shall not be hu-man but you shall become Man, the God Image within you! We operate at the fullest capacity of mental power here in our worlds, and this is probably the essential difference between our octave and yours, and our lives and your lives. Your lives can be changed for the better, toward perfection of all of your divine potential as Sons of God, if you will enter the study that will activate your sleeping splendor. I am Hatonn, and I urge each one of you to apply yourselves diligently with Love. The capacity would not be present if it were not your divine heritage."

George Hunt Williamson has said, "Science and religion are one and the same thing. God provided and man divided. There is no religion higher than truth. The entire Omniverse is magnetic in nature and even culture is effected by the higher laws of magnetism."

2. We are individually a little universe, a tiny speck of a greater vast Intelligence, and individually a portion of a tremendous power that is within us and surrounding us. This power has been called "God" by religion; science calls it "energy"; metaphysicians call it "Universal Mind" or "All That Is." I am not overly concerned about terminology since terminology is very limiting, so please do not become overly distressed by terminology.

As we refer to our sketch of "George" once more (refer to illustration on page 89), we notice that the cerebrum represents by far the greatest part of the bulk of the brain. It is four-fifths of the brain weight for which science can find no known function. They know it is not for thinking, not being a participating part of the cortex or the grey matter. We may use tensor terminology or awareness terminology, or whatever terminology is your personal preference. However, because the tensor terminology relates specifically to the dormancy of brain areas, it

THE IMPRISIONED SPLENDOR
(THE TENSOR CENTER)

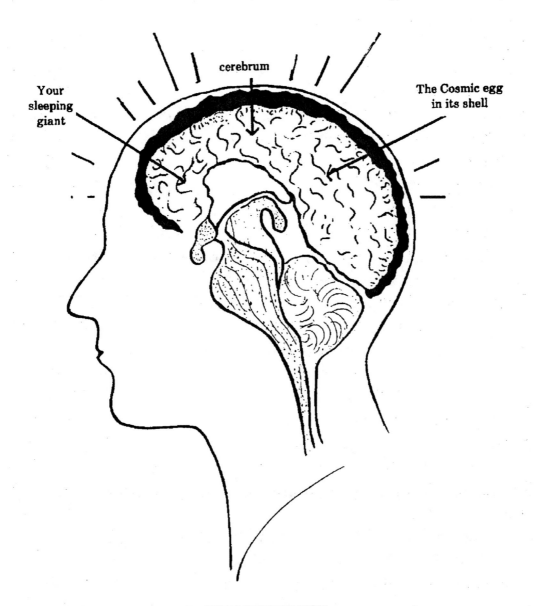

Your
sleeping
giant

cerebrum

The Cosmic egg
in its shell

THE GURU WITHIN YOU

gains importance. Since tensor has to do with potential for
thought retention, this in turn related to the potential for
increased numbers of synaptical junctions, which are the only
route for opening up a greater passageway between the cortex,
the cerebrum and the thalamus.

Nevertheless, let it be emphasized that essentially the thrust of the subject under discussion is *the awakening of the dormant four-fifths of the brain to its divine function in total human development.*

3. & 4. The cerebrum houses your sleeping giant of genius, your imprisoned glory and splendor, your cosmic egg of infinite intelligence and wisdom, your personal guru, and the center of your electromagnetic resonating power. This resonating center actually functions continually and never rests. It is here that thoughts from Universal Mind are nested through an inductive process, pulled through the resonating electromagnetic field surrounding the physical form. It then passes the thought on to the cortex for translation, application and action. Eventually in the highest spiritual development there will be a coordinated action between both the cerebrum and the cortex, the thought center and the thinking processes. Ultimately, through continual application of spiritual principles, development as a Light Being will bring forth this beautiful coordination. Remember this fact—the resonating center acts independent of any human thinking process, yet it is from here that all spiritual awareness comes and all inspired genius. It is the ultraconsciousness, the medium for all extrasensory phenomena. It is the connecting link with all heavenly beings and the seat of all parapsychic abilities. It is your personal light beam communicator, sending forth a frequency that resonates and resonates and resonates into infinity. We can strike a lower scale note of F on the piano key and listen as it resonates to the F note an octave above, and then to the F note an octave above that, and so on. So it is, that the quality of our projected frequency will resonate into the highest heavens only to rest when it is blended with that vibration to which is it attuned. Behind thought there is Intelligence, and Intelligence directs, such as in visualization. Mind is neutral—it *directs* the flow of action and energy.

At this point in my thinking, I was delighted to receive

these words from Aljanon relating to resonance:

4. "Within the terminology of science we find many parallels that will help us to understand the deeper significance of the universal principles that apply to mind resonance. Science speaks of energy, and resonance is moving energy, forging its pathway through the essence of living particles of Light. Science speaks of propulsion, and thought is propulsion of true energy as it flashes through the Universal substance toward its destination or point of rest. Within the combination of the two terms of energy propulsion it becomes a simple process to literally visualize the processes involved in telepathy. The propulsion principle acts in both directions. As one sits in mental openness to receive, they are projecting the energy of their desire and, at the same time, the sender is propelling the energy of thought-idea into the path of waiting desire."

"So you see that these two simple terms can make a very complex subject understandable to all. Science speaks of metabolism within the human body, which is nothing more than the individualized action and propulsion of each cell as it races on its way within the lifestream of a living soul, propelled by the ongoing life force, ever energized by the propulsion of the breath of life feeding the human brain. The metabolism is therefore slowed down in tempo as cells are commanded to lessen their pace when one desires pure mental action."

Thought resonance is the process of interaction between two diverse polarities—the positive sender and the negative receiver. Thought resonance is binding energy. I include here some further words received by Bob Renaud from his Space contacts:

"In line with telepathy and clairaudience, both are beyond the range of the normal senses and without electronic help. The All-Mind is brought in. Since it encompasses all, it is aware of everything that happens anywhere in the Universe. If a conscious mind should therefore wish to see at a distance, it need only work through the ultraconscious, requesting a view of a scene.

"On other occasions, the All-Mind may elect to provide this view unasked, and these are the 'sudden flashes' often heard about, even on your planet. For prescience, the All-Mind may project an image of what could very well occur if a certain pattern of events were to continue uninterrupted. In more cases than not, nothing much can be done about the sequence, so that the image therefore becomes a prediction."

5. The tensor centers actually are several, all interconnected. The cerebrum, the synapses, the thalamus, as well as the two master glands, all come under this category. The stimulation of all of these is involved in the tensor concepts which are concerned with their interaction under divine impetus, through the thalamatic pause, inciting tensor awakenings. But it is that great portion of white matter representing four-fifths of the brain area which primarily represents what we are calling the resonating tensor center. Aljanon has explained:

"The white matter is that portion of your brain which is the antenna for receiving messages from your I Am Presence by way of your Christ Self. When one is One with the Christ, this area glows with the Golden Color of Perfection."

Sometimes I find it hard to understand why there would not be some curiosity on the part of science regarding this supposedly useless mass of tissue. Yet if they were to search for its function they would, of necessity, be doing so through cortical action and therefore, be unsuccessful. They simply call it "the white matter" and let it go at that. Well, fasten your seatbelts, for here we go into something exciting as well as interesting.

Most of us who have studied spiritual matters at all are familiar with the importance of the spine in meditative activity. We have read of it as the vital path of the "kundalini"; in our meditations we have pulled the "golden white Light" down its direction to bathe the various chakras with the Light. We have been taught to sit with it as straight as possible and not to slump over, squeezing the solar plexus, but to maintain that spine straight as a rod of power. And why not? It is our personal caduceus coil—our very own tensor coil, if you please—wrapped in the two opposite winding poles of energy as symbolized in the "rod of Hermes." The spinal route interconnects all seven of the chakras in a dramatic fashion.

As I poured through heavy textbooks on loan from a neurologist friend and dug into stacks of encyclopedias, it was a real source of joy to me when I found that the same "white matter" which comprises the golden tensor center also follows down and comprises the center core of the spine! There is also a strip of white matter which wraps around the thalamus. A small segment of the spine shown in the sketch here shows the small bit of gray matter (G.M.) totally surrounded with a thick area of white matter (W.M.) which makes up the core of the spine. So we have learned that in the physical octave there is this connecting link between the seven chakras and the brain antenna system that links us with Universal Mind. Somehow, in ways we have yet to understand, penetrated into the fibers of this "white matter" are the genes that are the uniqueness of You and your connecting link with All That Is!

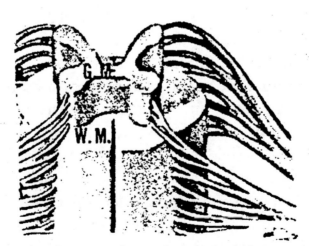

Segment of spinal cord, viewed from in front with portion of white matter removed and showing origin of spinal nerves.

"I will praise thee: for I am fearfully and wonderfully made...." (Psalms 139:14).

At birth we are automatically provided with natural communication equipment to achieve mental attunement or rapport with all intelligence anywhere in the Universe!

• • •

6. I have a very fine dictation received from Athena, on Ashtar's Starship, in which she tells us of the Synthascan which turns our thoughts into color images. She discusses the use of the tensor beam, the act of receiving, and the overshadowing of great Masters:

"The mind is a vacuum that attracts unto itself that which surrounds it in terms of electrical impulses. It then manipulates these impulses until they are born as Thought. Through brain processes this then becomes idea, then action. We monitor this process on screens that are designed for this purpose. The quality of the thinking taking place is reflected in color and the intensity is evident in the tone of that color. We do not become involved with words in this process. Our monitoring equipment is a revelator in the same manner that the human aura reveals information without the use of words.

"As telepathic communication is in process a beam from one of our ships—if that is the source of the contact—beams into and blends with the human aura surrounding the individual. The electrical impulses of the one who sends are captured within the electronic field surrounding the receiver and the thought-idea is filtered to the tensor center of the brain. The receiver then converts the thought-idea into words, yet much help is present in this also. For often in the case of one well practiced in this activity, distinct words will be received for transcription."

A tensor beam is directed toward a group, a location, or an individual who is directly in line with a ship of whatever size that is directly overhead. In many many cases our great

94

leaders will be sending their communication from another point, which is then relayed to a smaller ship in the area of the communicant from which the beam is used. *There is always present in the area of our earth representatives, a fleet member who stands by* in the cooperative service with our embodied one, ever monitoring, ever guarding, ever guiding and relaying the guidance of others to the one who serves with us. You are never alone. This network becomes the All-Seeing Eye of the Heavenly Father.

"The personal thought world of those who receive is set aside and the mind is stilled from its personal activity. Its full attention is focused upon that one who awaits in the heavens or in the shadows as the case may be. With the physical form and the brain held in stillness and silence of inner peace, one who stands ready to send can then enter the thought transference process. You are 'hearing,' rather, receiving each distinct word that I am relaying to you, There are other times when only the thought idea is given. In the latter we are often limited by a halting vocabulary or a lack in the inherent ability to express fluently. We prefer the direct sending of the verbal message when clear reception makes this possible. However, there are many considerations involved which will often render this unsuccessful. Some of these considerations are extreme tiredness of the receiver, illness, weather, and electrical interference or other disturbances, including physical circumstances and even emotional upsets within the receiver's environment. The finest of channels often have their days when the telepathic thread is not as powerful as it is at other times. It is not my purpose at this time to discuss these many factors; nevertheless, we do desire to clarify some existing discrepancies in information.

"The Great Masters who overshadow their chelas with their own force-field are not using a tensor beam in the sense that it is used by the Confederation members. The Beloved Brotherhood will often project their Being near the physical form of their student and directly filter their thoughts into the waiting mind of the chela, blending the two force-fields. In either case, the disciplines and qualifications for this spiritual communication are the same, whether one is receiving through tensor beaming or direct projection.

"Words will appear to march across the mental screen like the action of the ticker tape. The receiving soul *must be detached* from that which is projected, *not identifying with the content or confusing it with the thinking process of human rationalization.* One must not attempt to discern where the message is leading or to discern its destination. Intellect and reasoning *will sever the telepathic thread.* When the message has been written or typed, or otherwise recorded, then the intellect may consider and discern its content through the thinking process, but not before. Until the transcription is completed, *human reasoning must give way to SOUL FORCE in quiet passivity.*

"Under the watchful authority of the Spiritual Hierarchy, this vast protective scanning is ever carried on in fulfilling the promises that have been made to the children of Light. Humanity has now progressed in its technological awareness that provides a frame of understanding the position of the Space Armada in the divine scheme of things. Highly advanced technology makes our communications with you an accomplished reality, free of the bigoted connotations once associated with it by the ignorant masses.

"The deeper your scientific community penetrates into research on the human brain and the electricity of the human form, the greater will be the falling away of inhibiting concepts clothed in religious dogma. Cosmic Telepathy is a reality, proven again and again through many cultures and civilizations and it is the driving force in the present renaissance of understanding and awakening that must come to humanity before its midnight hour has come. I am Athena, in joint command with Ashtar of Starship 10 of this hemisphere."

• • •

In response to my direct request, our science editor, Richard Woodmaster, has submitted the following explanation of the tensor beam, its divisions and manifestations:

"Primarily, the tensor beam energizes new synaptical connections to the unused centers of the brain, thereby integrating the human nervous system and the emotional and physical control centers. As a result, the individual emanates a special radiation in large amounts, which makes telepathic communication possible. The tensor beam specifically is for *assisting* this person in their telepathy!

7. "The tensor beam is comprised of a three-phase magnetic carrier wave, projected in a cone-shaped field of radiation, tuned to the precise frequency of the individual who is to receive the signal. These three components are: a core surrounded by the two concentric tubular layers of magnetic substance. The central core is a phase standing columnar wave of radiation two inches in diameter which, when projected, acts on the brain of the receiving person. The inner tubular layer controls the immediate physical environment and extends four inches beyond the body area. The outer tubular layer contains a return circuit, which picks up the emanations from the minds of anyone in close proximity to the receiving person, returning their thoughts upon this carrier to monitors onboard hovering spacecraft. These monitors (Somnivision, Synthascan, etc.) detect, amplify, and display these wave components upon screens for studying and recording.

"Our thought is what actuates the tensor beam equipment. Thus, two-way communication is possible even though the three-phase carrier wave is generated at one end of the system only. When the receiving body is in resonance with the carrier wave, a small but adequate portion of the audio signal will be generated upon the auditory nerve and several other nerves which extend to various parts of the body but terminate in or near the auditory center of the brain. The end result is, the individual on the receiving end 'hears' the spoken word in the same way as though the original sound waves were reaching his ears.

"The watching, listening, and communicating equipment is combined by the use of sending this very highly vibrational light beam through a projector lens. This beam is a penetrating ray of light which can go through objects and matter, so that all can be seen indoors as well as out, by tuning out roofs and walls, so to speak.

"The tensor beam system is similar to a radar system, in that a wave is emitted in a certain direction by a beam transmitter. Any thought energy or object in the path of the wave will reflect a portion of it back toward the transmitter. These return signal components are then picked up by transmitting unit, amplified and displayed upon a viewing screen for study.

"In principle, the tensor beam is a multi-purposed beam, utilized for influence of those to whom it is projected, and for surveillance as well."

I do hope that his good explanation will clarify your understanding as it did mine!

● ● ●

Some persons experience various characteristics when the tensor beam is placed upon them. They tell of nausea, a feeling of a tight band or pressure around the head, abdominal cramps at the solar plexus area. Others have mentioned a quickening of the heart chakra, a trembling, or a swaying or shaking of the body. Depending on the individual's vibration rate, some experience heat, some cold. There may be a tingling nervousness, or extreme excitement, or perhaps "goose bumps" or sweating.

In any case, physical effects are simply the results of a frequency adjustment, not harmful and very temporary. Anyone in close physical proximity to the receiver of a tensor beam, holding hands, or near their vibrational force-field, may actually pick up the same physical effects.

The presence of this beam upon us stimulates chakra and

glandular areas of activity and considerably increases the body frequency, thus assisting the telepath. In almost all cases, the moment the physical effects have passed and total passivity is present, the communication begins. In my own experiences, when the normal beam is accelerated to a higher frequency than is normally used, for whatever reason, the physical form vibrates as in a vortex and resonates so forcibly there is a resonating tone in the head area. All of this quickly passes, and I know the Speaker is ready to begin.

• • •

We have hitherto had so much to say about Cosmic Communications, it seems only fitting that we should mention one very key person in all of these matters. I speak of Commander KORTON, who is Director of Space Communications for our Solar System and Commander of Starship Rainbow. The main communications center, which is his responsibility, is called KOR and is located upon the planet Mars.

There they have available every possible kind of communications available, but he states (through spiritual messenger, White Dove), "...our fastest communication is telepathy and the tensor beam, which we use at all times."

No more than a dozen or so persons are needed to efficiently operate KOR's communications center. This great relay station channels 7000 messages simultaneously from one destination to another. Every message we receive from a higher being or send to celestial realms goes through station KOR, relayed instantaneously as well as recorded and filed. The same can be said of all monitored material, thus making the words of our Beloved who referred to "every jot and tittle" being preserved, far easier to comprehend. I personally, on many occasions when I desire to reach a certain personage, will contact KOR and Commander Korton direct and ask him to "patch me through" quickly to so-and-so if the emergency is an urgent one. There is seldom more than a few moments wait and that one will respond. So do let us give expression of our gratitude to Beloved Korton, who serves all of this universal sector so admirably and efficiently in this aspect of cosmic communications.

• • •

There are, quite evidently, some blessed souls to whom telepathy comes easier than it does to others. At some point in certain individuals' lives, certain experiences will "trigger" a communications link and recall of various degrees takes place.

Through the scanning equipment on monitoring spacecraft, a certain radiating emanation is detected around these persons. When this fact is automatically noted by the surveying craft, the individual is closely watched and, if needful, cosmic communication takes place.

• • •

I have an informative message from Sector Commander Andromeda Rex in which he touches upon the distinction between telepathy and trance methods, among other things.

"The audible word that you hear in telepathy, while not really audible, is actually an impression that is made upon the mind of the receiver. It is a mental thread that holds two minds in communication with one another. And so it is, that my mind and yours are fused together at this moment through our mutual frequency. Your telepathic ability is not something that is developed or expanded; it is discovered, as a natural function of the brain which has had accustomed use in other lifetimes. Therefore, it flows freely in this one because of past usage.

"There is that portion in the human brain which is almost never used, which is capable of tremendous scope of activity which we accelerate through the use of our tensor beam placed upon our participants, which enables these idle areas to become exercised and active.

10. "In the case of our spiritual messengers and representatives, we have found telepathy to be a great improvement

over the trance type of transmission. In that nature of communication, the participant is unaware of that which is transferred through him. In the use of consciously cooperating channels a more perfect record can be kept of that transaction, even when alone. Further, the translation into the vernacular of the messenger flows much smoother than the often inarticulate and harshness of the use of the human voice box through trance. Many still use that method with much success, but we have found that for these latter day events, the telepathic method is more efficient and not depleting to our messengers, for a message may need to be transcribed hurriedly and instantly and not necessarily under seance conditions, making this type more versatile in emergency situations. Therefore, we have chosen to institute telepathic communication on a broad scale, not only as the communication method in our worlds, but also as that chosen method for the cleansing period on earth. There are hundreds of persons now in the process of entering into a telepathic experience through their meditations and contacts with us. These are being activated quickly to be useful to the Commands in that hour of dire emergency, within family and group situations.

"In the studies of science concerning the human brain, telepathy has already been accepted as an actual function of the human brain and much research has been accomplished. This will go forward at an accelerated speed, along with our assisting beams to earth to expand its use."

• • •

By this time, it is hoped that by sheer repetition some of the telepathic principles have become lodged in your cortex. Many of our fine messengers in this book have, of a necessity, had to overlap one another in discussing their subject. In closing this chapter, there is one more speaker to be heard: Commander Anton, formerly of Cook Mountain Station near here, and now on a world tour of duty, who is Master of Energy and

Geometrics, Nuclear Physics, and various other distinguished accomplishments. I appreciated the way he linked the principles of telepathy with the principle of propulsion of their spacecraft:

11. "There is no difference in the action of the human brain as propelled by mind, than that same propulsion of our ships. We also use the mind to activate all important action within the highly technical movement of our own navigation through space.

"The action of mind steps up the atoms of living energy in a direct pulsation which manifests as energy that propels. When a powerful thought injection is received from outer space through the magnetic resonating field of the individual and enters into the thinking process of the human brain, action has been initiated by another mind to the mind which now receives it. It is as fallible and dependable in the directives of mind to mind contact as it is when propelling our craft through space. Projected thought is fierce in its speed and its power, as well as its penetrating ability. One must *know* this to be true for it to be true! As a man thinketh, so it is for that man.

"The millions of tiny nerve cells that are housed in the resonating sector of the brain where all invisible perception takes place, act as tiny receiving stations or as crystals, through which the power of thought is propelled forward into the waiting cerebrum, there to be transformed into ideas, words or pictures to be thrown upon the picture screen of the thalamus. This entire process operates smoothly and efficiently *as long as the action of the thinking brain is held in abeyance* through this activity.

"When piercing the distance of space to send a message, a call, a name of a certain one, the process is reversed as the cerebrum projects its missile of thought through the electromagnetic resonating forcefield of the human brain into Universal Mind surrounding it. From there it is immediately registered in the atoms of space, ever resonating, ever moving forward until it rests in the proper frequency of the being to whom it is directed—an invisible thread of direct thought communication between those that call and those that answer.

"It is preferable to know whom you are addressing and specifically calling, than to eject a general call; for definiteness of call brings definiteness of response. It is well to realize also that when a certain one is called, that one may at that moment be occupied with important activities of another nature that temporarily may take priority. In that case, the caller will usually be advised of this or instructed to pause in the vibration until the called one is free to respond. If impossible, an appointment will be set up. If no such problem is present, the response will be instantaneous. The use of definite appointments with busy individuals is a very wise procedure."

—Anton

I was told that those selected hours divisible by three, such as 3:00, 6:00, 9:00 and 12:00, were the most favorable.

As Commander Anton withdraws, let us close our thinking upon his words with a brief summary of the propulsion process in telepathy:

12. A. Universal Mind is the connecting link between all minds;

   B.—Projecting as a Force through the human aura as its avenue of cosmic impulse;

   C.—Entering into the resonating cerebrum (tensor) sector as pure thought energy;

   D.—Going from there to the thalamus as symbol or picture, and then to the cortex converted to words, thinking and action.

Think on These Things

1. What is the greater gift to be found within the quest to master Cosmic Telepathy?
2. Give three terms for Universal Power.
3. Name five terms to describe the cerebrum, and locate it within the total brain.
4. Can you describe "thought resonance"?
5. Name the tensor centers.
6. Explain the process of Syntha-scan.
7. Define the three parts of the tensor beam.
8. Discuss some of the physical effects of the tensor beam.
9. What is K O R?
10. Distinguish between telepathy and trance.
11. What is meant by thought propulsion and how does it relate to space ship navigation?
12. Discuss the four stages of the propulsion process in telepathy.

NOTES:

Part III
Discipline

IX
The Dynamics of Technique

1. Kuthumi has given us this statement to open Part Three: "Discipline is born in discipleship; it is its hallmark. The disciple understands the place of discipline. There are many disciplines, and many new ones are added as the chela progresses upon the pathway. The attainment of higher awareness demands a continuing consistency and constancy in the application of discipline backed by desire. Spiritual hunger, fostered by a determination to use the gift for the benefit of others and the advancement of Light upon the planet, is the proper approach. One must not take this lightly; it is the individual's spiritual heritage. It is the unfoldment of the inner splendor. It is the goal of humanity and is not intended for entertainment or the parading of personal prowess in certain areas. Those who speak most often of their humility seldom are. The spiritual attainments are vehicles of service to mankind and unless one seeks within that discipline and motivation, one seeks in vain."

2. The goal in technique is a trained intelligent cooperation, a lessening of density, a change of specific gravity. Technique, or knowledge, is after all, only information. Any amount of knowledge will accomplish nothing unless it is absorbed and applied.

A teacher at the college level who is adept in the highly advanced computer mathematics would not be positioned at a first grade level to render the secrets of 1+1=2. So, likewise, during your most basic and fundamental early training, do *not* expect continual attention and daily technique instructions from the Archangel ranks! They may, at vastly isolated times, pop in to keep you inspired, but *do* expect your early nitty-gritty training to have some very wise and beautiful teachers from the less prominent levels of Hierarchal structure. As you advance, newer teachers will replace your basic training instructors, who will know exactly when you are ready to be introduced to a higher level of approach. Do not become a *name dropper* in the etheric sense. In your early beginnings if too much importance is attached to names, you will overlook *content* and even invite imposters. Do realize that this heavenly personnel will constantly be changing as you advance in knowledge, wisdom and understanding, along with your burning desire for attainment.

In more cases than not, the identity of your various instructors may be related to a former soul tie or a relationship with the individual which makes a telepathic thread with that one easier for you by past association and link, than it might be with another. But nevertheless, they will still withdraw and be replaced by higher teachers who, again, may have a soul tie of some nature with you. From each dimensional source those will be found who work best with you.

For a very long period, one whom history remembers as Herodotus was one of my own prominent teachers. A very scholarly and meticulous teacher he was, yet loving and gentle and utterly understanding and patient with his stumbling student. But later, when I found out the details of our long-ago relationship, so much fell into place to help me understand. Eventually his work with me was finished, and he turned me over to another. The soul whom the world knows as Apostle Peter, or just Peter, identifies himself as the "voice of the Mystics," and at some time undoubtedly he will also take a turn in the preparing of a new chela. Korton and Monka also both do much work in the assistance to new messengers.

Because of a long working association with Jesus the Christ, as a minister and Christian mystic, He became the one to introduce me into personal contact with the other Great Masters and Chohans. It was Jesus himself who introduced me to Kuthumi and Hilarion, thereby removing any sense of uneasiness in the flow of contact. As close as my relationship with Kuthumi proved to be—now and in ages past—it took this personal touch from Jesus to facilitate my launching into new Hierarchal areas. Then, in turn, Master Kuthumi introduced me to the Space Confederation Commanders, introducing a new phase of discipleship and responsibility.

• • •

Consistently, the first emphasis in the general disciplines has to do with scheduling a time for spiritual upreach. One should have a personally chosen time of day for this exercise when any form of interruption is unlikely. Take the phone off the hook, for the sudden jarring ringing will have a violent effect upon one in deep meditation. Your friends will call back later; for the moment, your Cosmic telephone takes precedence. This is your hour with God, so plan and prepare for uninterrupted quietness, however short the period may need to be. A split-second interruption can cause misinterpretation of the impression. Impressions fly through the mind at great speed. The more disinterested we become in ourselves as a personal ego, the finer our perceptions become.

In the quiet place of the inner citadel, apart from the noises of earth-life, there one must retreat daily to hear the still small voice of the Christ Presence. Indulging in some form of spiritual and inspirational reading is helpful in preparing for prayer with the Heavenly Father, or a certain quality of a favorite musical recording can lift the soul in preparation for attunement. Questions that you have should be prepared before and kept near you. They will be seen, and if there is time, you will be invited to offer them.3. Do realize that there is every possibility that you are here on a voluntary assignment to the planet. The daily appointments always at the same time builds an enforcement of protection around you made up of those Beings assigned to your life stream for instruction and protection. The appointment is a method of enforcing this protection. You are also protected by your own integrity and purpose, but the presence of your Guardians is the dominant factor. For the beginner and student, haphazard and impromptu contacts can sometimes let in the unexpected and uninvited. (Details on proper attunement procedures will follow in the next chapter).

4. Further, there will be many times, doubtless, when you will feel that your time of stillness was unproductive and a waste of time. Do not believe this, for your teachers will tell you that in every moment spent with them, something productive is happening, for much interaction takes place in the physical form, the electromagnetic field, and on spiritual levels. If there "seems" to have been no results, ignore that, and admit at least that the rest has been good for you! But in the center core of being, *KNOW* that your faithfulness has been observed. Athena has said, "Keep the appointments even though you may consider them a waste of time. It is important for us to know that you have appeared, whether transmission is accomplished or not. We will be the best judge of that. Be prompt and faithful in your part of the agreement. There is a mystical reason for this."

5. Continuing with Kuthumi's words, he also cautions: "Punctuality and the keeping of appointed times is an important discipline. If one cannot keep an appointment, send forth that message into Universal Mind. It shows respect and courtesy, and is appreciated. When one can be faithful—and there is not a reasonable reason for being otherwise—then keep the appointment. This builds within you a sense of discipline that expands its blessings into all the areas of life. Each time the

chela is faithful in the smaller things, the action reveals *a capacity* for responsibility in the greater things.

"Self discipline leads the disciple into deeper and deeper initiations after initiations along the pathway to Mastery. Nevertheless, as you come into new embodiments, all of the former attainment must be brought through, pulled through, the human consciousness. The striving is less, the attainment is easier than it may be for others, but the discipline is still present and brings the results, even for those with great spiritual heritage in their soul records. As you reach and as you desire, so shall you receive."

• • •

6. There are disciplines of breath followed by many, and ignored by others. Follow your own intuition and personal comfort regarding these things. Breathing exercises are very relaxing to the taut physical form. A teacher once told me, before I had entered into any reading on such things: "When the body is quiet and relaxed, take into thyself three very long breaths, holding them within for a long period, and very slowly again, exhaling the breaths with the mouth open. Repeat this exercise three times and then stop. The vibrating sideways motion will have begun and you will know that communication may be begun." Many prefer to combine this exercise with the sounding of the holy OHM while exhaling the breath. This may be done three or nine times before attunement.

It is said that the breath is the cord that ties the mind to the body. If a man is restless his breath is restless, and when he is calm, his breath is almost non-perceptive. Breath and mind are closely related, and in approaching meditation, calming the breath calms the mind as well as the heart. One source suggests counting to eight when breathing in and counting to eight when breathing out.

• • •

There are diets, and diets, and more diets, and were we to attempt to please everyone else we would be, of all souls, most miserable. Plainly you must find your own pace and your own suitable eating pattern. I offer here a series of suggestions that from time to time have allegedly come from spiritual sources, for you to weigh in the balances.

Agreement seems to be rather widespread that coming to the meditation time immediately after having partaken of heavy food drags heavily upon the upper glands. It is recommended that at least for two full hours before the meditation time, heavy foods be forsaken. Fortunately, one does not have to believe this; simply experiment with it and you will know it forever by the results. Further, it has been repeatedly requested that one not partake of any alcoholic beverages for three hours before meditation, since these create a disrupted metabolism which affects the vibrations. Sweets, foods overly rich in fats, and overeating of breads are frowned upon by Peter, the teacher of the mystics, and many other higher ones. Dark breads are approved unless there is a tendency present to overeat them.

When the conditioning of a spiritual messenger is in an intense period or beams are being intensified upon that one, almost all bulk needs to be removed. When transmissions are extremely intensified, in the interest of sheer bodily comfort, food had best be taken sparingly. Powerful jolts of resonating power passing through the body can build up until dizziness and nausea will be present. A heavy diet must not be present where intensified beam work is the schedule. Actually, at such times a liquid diet is recommended for avoiding any physical discomfort. My own contacts are the most intensified in the week prior to full moon, and I have accepted a discipline of extremely light eating at those times.

7. I bring in here another small portion of Cosmic Teacher Aljanon's message: "Those who desire to increase awareness of their Godself must eliminate certain food items from their

diets. The God Energies cannot work well through a cluttered body. The following foods are not conducive to bringing in higher energies into the physical plane. These are listed in the order of their importance: sugar, caffeine, alcohol, drugs of any sort, red meats and organ meats, herbs of garlic and onions, and certain black tea varieties. Become aware of the harmful effects that sugar, caffeine and alcohol have on your higher bodies. That is why they have been infiltrated into your lifestyles to such a degree."

We are also warned by Kuthumi against making too much haste in changing a diet pattern of a lifetime: "A slow process of changing the intake of foods, gradually dropping the ones that are most harmful, and gradually adding or increasing those that are most beneficial. Gradually drop the foods that have been processed to the point where the nutrition is no longer present, and slowly substituting the fresh fruits and vegetables and those things that are ready in their natural form. Progressively begin the purification of your body temple. This is an important discipline in the spiritual quest. Help is given as souls seek to help themselves in the body purification. Material is placed in those hands and helps are sent as guidance. This, again, is a discipline. Drop off the commercial tea and begin to substitute with the healing herbs and their teas. Drop off the flesh of animals as you are enabled to. Do not attempt to do it suddenly. Begin first by dropping of the flesh of swine; then, when that is an accepted routine, drop the red meats. Simply determine in your mind that you will begin this effort in a small way, gradually, until finally you will have purified the form by giving it only the purest foods of mother earth—the nuts, the grains, the fruits, the vegetables, the blowing wheat, continuing with the supplements as desired."

8. Another teacher, while discussing a long list of various helpful hints, mentioned clothing: "Be unhindered by those items of clothing which would bind the body so as to draw attention to itself. Comfort is needed. Let the body be loosely

clothed. Total relaxation of all the physical attributes is the essence of pushing the soul foremost. The body warreth against the spirit, and the body must be subdued. Let it also be clean and free of bodily sweats and soils or food upon the mouth. The aromas of earth are repulsive to higher beings." Well, there you have it, ladies...off with the girdles and on with the mu-mus. Why not rip up a good, white sheet and create for yourself a prayer toga and use it for nothing else. Try this and see how good it feels! Fellows, unbutton the shirt neck, remove your belt and shoes, or perhaps now you can use that bathrobe your mother-in-law gave you last Christmas...or maybe you can find a white *cotton* terry robe to keep for your attunement times. You also will enjoy the feeling that comes to you from feeling the white surrounding your form. The same teacher closed with these words: "Let there be a total relaxation of the physical body as is necessary to communication, and let there be an expectancy of response. Maintain a positive attitude of mind, that what is sought will be forthcoming."

The teacher quoted above scarcely left a stone unturned in the long list of general hints on various items. For what it is worth, I will add on three more. The first one seems rather important, having to do with the purifying of the mind:

"Refrain from having within your home anything of printed nature that would detract the soul from its occupation with the things that are for the soul development. Degenerate literatures and fruits of the modern press should not be fed into one's mind, but rather, give the time to pursuing such things as are designed for spiritual development. Guidance will be forthcoming in finding these literatures to be studied faithfully and diligently by the disciple."

He also calls for an attitude that prevents the entry of worry and anxiety:

"The life of faith learns to rest in Divine provision for all earthly needs while consecrating health and well-being to the service of the Light. For one cannot serve two masters; neither can ye serve mammon and spiritual progress. Present your bodies as living sacrifices, to be filled, to be refined, for the use of the Light."

Finally, he very adroitly discriminates better from best:

"The dedicated life faces many diversionary avenues which tend to draw one away from spiritual determinations. Learn to *discern between that which is good and that which is better, that you might remain your best FOR THE SERVICE OF THE KINGDOM.* To this end, the inner level chela must guard against occupation with worldly pursuits, though seeming to be good works, would make inroads into that which is best. Let not yourself become entangled in the affairs of others to the extent that your own soul would suffer, but seek first the will of the Father in those matters."

After having placed all of these admonitions before you concerning the physical form, let us now hear the last word on the matter, which comes to us from ORPHIEL, of the 12th sphere of manifestation, speaking from the Celestial region of the Great Central Sun:

"In the metaphysical mystique concerning interdimensional transference of thought, too much emphasis has been placed upon bodily function or a lack of bodily function. In reality, cosmic telepathy is concerned only with mind-to-mind resonating frequencies.

9. "One may say the body must be quieted in this or that position or this or that disengagement, when actually the resonating magnetism of two minds meeting on the Universal frequency can very easily take place while one is driving a vehicle, or walking in a crowd, or waiting for an elevator! The mind can create its own inner citadel anytime, anywhere, in any situation. The criterion is the completion of the frequency contact and not of bodily posture or the lack of it. So be cautious not to create bondage or complication where none exists!

"The resonating center of the human brain is designed to let flow through it the Universal telepathic frequency when it is allowed to do so. It is already serving you in this capacity; you need only to step aside from its pathway by decelerating conscious thought. The windows of heaven flood Light through the tensor sectors, allowing them to resonate in great force if the cerebral actions surrounding the brain are commanded to halt their human interference! Learn to visualize the various sections of the brain and proceed from one to another, commanding them to be still and not distract you from the intuitive flow that you do consciously invite to flood your tensor areas.

"Universal Mind, or Spirit, is already totally familiar with every detail that concerns your embodiment and service. You need not talk incessantly of these things to Higher Consciousness. Whatever flows in will be exactly what you need most to hear, and its pertinence will astound you! You must let this flow through you of its own volition. Do not labor or struggle to forcefully pull it through. Simply be still, resting quietly in your love and confidence in the Father and letting that pure love resonate through you. Effortlessly surround your world and solar system, caring not for results nor preconceiving any outcome—simply basking in your own inner peace. Then the rivers of Life will flood your being."

• • •

10. Perhaps we should consider here some of the physical effects that may appear. Rest assured that all higher contact vibrations help and cleanse the body. They pass through the mental body harmlessly, because that is its function. It is the source of communication on other planes. Physical effects vary with individuals. There may be an electronic sound in the ear, or one may hear a noise like a rushing wind, in rare cases. There may be a weaving of the body, or a feeling of the body floating above its chair or couch. Whether one sits or stands; or reclines on a bed, the floor, or a chair, makes no difference. However, it is good, some say, to have the spine straight. The presence of a spacecraft may produce an electronic sound in

your head, though not necessarily. For a considerable length of time I would hear a clickety-click in my right ear when communication was desired—a kind of calling or alerting signal. Now a different system is used. You are a unique individual, and all of your experiences may be totally different from those of another. It is not important. For a period of time, in my own meditations, whenever a message was about to be given, side to side weaving vibrations increased, combined with a deepening purple color; then both would gradually decline as the message ended. As they receded, this would be followed by an increase once more, as a further statement was given. It reminded me of the incoming and outgoing waves of the ocean, reaching a crest every seventh wave. Early in my training, when I fully returned to the physical consciousness, I would feel sleepy and would yawn considerably. I wanted to throw myself on the bed and nap a bit, but then the inclination would suddenly leave me.

I would be pleased to share with you some of the sittings with my Teachers as a determined dedicated beginning student. I was located deep into a rural area beyond city access to any groups or classes, and all of my spiritual training came directly from Spirit in one to three daily appointments of quietness with them. This was as much as nine years ago. I was seeking an explanation one day of the peculiar weavings of the physical form, and they answered: "We are increasing your mental faculty to adjust to our presence in your magnetic field. Our vibrational penetration creates the increase in body vibrations. A side-to-side effect indicates we are present and very close within the energy field. Do not resist this action, for it is involved in our approach to you. When the vibration is circular of motion, it indicates that we need a few more moments for accustomedness and are not quite ready. Just wait for the side-to-side motion, which indicates readiness. Learn that without this vibration you are to continue to wait and not receive. A downward pull or motion indicates that we are ready for the typing to begin. A lifting up pull or backward motion indicates that the communication is coming to a close."

11. "Colors are caused by the aura's excitement in raising the vibration. The coming of higher Beings to blend with a human aura will always produce beautiful colors. The particular color is not so important as the fact that it is there. Perfect faith and trust will usually produce blue; the purple indicates a deeper state of relaxation. Deep pinks are the effect of the Light surrounding us blending with the Light around you; and the same applies to the pure yellow. These are the living colors of the living souls surrounding your own soul colors."

All of heaven is a blaze of beautiful color; even our clothing is only color, and we take into ourselves through a field of color. It sustains us and is our breath of spiritual life. We break down color into its various prisms, and each different one gives us sustenance and energy. Color is the vibratory medium of the Universe. We correlate all color together when we gather and it is beautiful to behold. The absence of color, or a very dark or deep tone, is an indication of lower vibrations which need to ascend. Indigo blue is perhaps the purest indication of high spirituality and aspiration. You need never fear to trust anyone who is surrounded in the purest blue. Greens are well, but it is a weaker vibration, and when higher souls blend with it, it becomes blue. Colors are visual manifestations of Universal energies which surround all of us. Sit for color treatments, whether you are led to type or not."

It is important for the chela to keep a notebook of experiences, if only to shake in the face of the enemy when he comes as an accuser! I am quoting from one of my early entries concerning a routine 12:00 appointment with the Teachers:

"Today when I entered the silence and relaxed my body, they told me we would try a new discipline today. I could feel my spiritual self being lifted...climbing, reaching, higher...and higher...and higher. I could sense myself just sitting up there (like suspended animation), way, way up there, for some reason which hopefully they would explain. I knew it was some kind of exercise and hoped I would not 'fall.' My fingers were twitching. Finally, I asked them what they were doing, anyhow! They said they were trying to move my fingers (that was obvious!) Then they said they would try to move my tongue, but it only seemed to tingle nervously. They said they would move my toes, but there was not any reaction at all.

"Then they asked me to select a favorite flower. That was easy and quick, since a yellow rosebud is my favorite of them all. They asked me to visualize a yellow rosebud, then bring it toward my nose for its fragrance, but I'm a pretty dense character—I didn't smell a thing! Then I was instructed, from now on, to construct—visualize—my yellow rosebud whenever I entered deep meditation as part of the spiritual exercise, because that would now become my personal psychic symbol as a yellow-ray soul.

"Following this, I was permitted, very very slowly, to let myself down again, which I did, and they continued to coach me to do so slowly...slowly. I came back to sensation and gradually stretched myself and yawned heavily, as usual! Meantime, they were saying, 'There will be many mental exercises such as this one to strengthen your mental faculty—primarily to stimulate the imagination, which is the primary weapon of the spiritual aspirant. When the imagination is working its instinctual powers, the spiritual self is released to its flowering activities. Imagination is also the mind of the soul, *the source of all true inspiration.*'"

Entries for the following days reveal my work with the rose with varying results. One entry reports: "I visualized my yellow rosebud as I had been told to do. I constructed it imaginatively before my closed eyes, but it was very faint and seemed to float around uncontrollably in a bed of vacillating purple. Occasionally my faith rose would come in close to me, and then withdraw or float away, but at times I could distinctly see its petals, and I thought, 'Oh how lovely it is,' Once when I was looking at it very plainly, they intruded,...'very good!' At that period of time, these moments would still be occasionally interrupted with things of earth life *forcing themselves* back in, intruding on my mental exercise. When I would realize what was taking place, I would hastily reconstruct my yellow rosebud. Then the Teacher spoke: 'This little bud will be your symbol of our presence with you. It represents our faithfulness to you and your loyalty to us, a symbol of our relationship and our work together. This exercise strengthens your concentration faculties.'"

This seemingly unrelated trivia was important because in the training it was strengthening mental faculties which, in time, would directly contribute to productive telepathic activity.

● ● ●

In the above passage it can be readily seen that the employment of the symbol (yellow rosebud) was used with me because it possessed the mental imprint of the Teacher to be communicated with. For me it established a firm tuning-in frequency and nothing more, yet an important link in the transaction. Before I learned to receive at my typewriter I had written the messages that came through Mind, and at the closing, a symbol was drawn through my hand which I later, much much later, learned was the Symbol of the Solar Cross, an equal armed cross enclosed in a circle. At that time it was their identity symbol to me. It is still used, sometimes "drawn" by the weaving of the physical form. To quote verbatim from Beloved Korton, through spiritual messenger Richard Miller (in *Star Wards*, now out of print):

12. "A symbol allows the fixing of one's telepathic attention on the thoughts of the telepathic communicant. Symbols play an important part in the transition of thought, from the levels of thought alone, into that which you call the material world. Symbols act as a conversion device whereby a thought can manifest itself in the physical world. They are an operative tool of the mind. The mind creates a thought. A symbol

becomes the tool employed by the mind to translate that thought. Conversely, anything that exists in the physical can be translated, through the means of a symbol, into the realm of thought."

Symbols can be pictures—not even real ones, but pictures constructed of words. In this case, we sometimes call them parables. Jesus the Christ was a Master in this type of symbol, or word picture. I like to think of it this way: a symbol is the means for pulling our concept of the known into the unknown, or vice versa. The symbol or picture gives us a *familiar* tool with which we can venture into that which we do not know or understand, and thereby through simple association, proceed to an understanding of the *unknown*. And so it was, that in discussing profound truths of the Kingdom of God, Jesus the Christ would begin with a lost coin out of sight, feverishly sought; or a priceless pearl concealed in a pasture, which inspired the pasture's purchase; or the decomposition of a grain of corn, leading to full maturity in four stages of development. So He began "where they were" and took them through the journey of thought to realms beyond their understanding. He would picture a plough in fallow ground, or a rock-strewn field, or good rich soil, to deepen an understanding of the human heart and its spiritual desire or lack of it. So often, to this Great Master, a field would represent the world, and a seed would represent the Truth, and all of us immediately understood! In this sense, a symbol is a window for letting in Light!

Many telepaths receive their material in symbol form, and it transports them into its proper application. Do not pass your symbols along to the receiver; they are yours to interpret, not the one to whom they are sent. You are equipped; perhaps they are not. The symbol helps you to find your way to the message or its reality, and is then discarded.

Many of us have pictures or paintings of the Higher Masters and Beings, and members of the Space Confederation.

These pictures (or symbols) are *not* the persons, but they *do* assist to fix our telepathic attention on the thoughts of that particular selected communicant. I often use this method when a certain appointment is in process or a call is being sent. The picture serves as a symbol, or tool, in my contact with that individual.

One more brief reference and we will be ready to move on into the steps of attunement. You will be forever a student, ever learning and exploring new vistas of awareness. Avoid slumping into a disciplined ritual! Do keep up the flow of eager spontaneous freshness. Flee from self-consciousness. After many many months of floundering on blind instinct, you will suddenly become saturated, permeated with the fluid strength of inspirational cosmic telepathy. Have faith in your effort and know that the only true relaxation is in accustomedness.

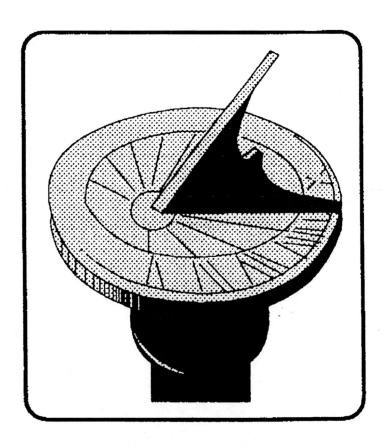

Think on These Things

1. What is the hallmark of discipleship?
2. What is the goal of technique in cosmic telepathy?
3. Do the same Teachers remain with a student for his entire embodiment?
4. What is the importance of a regular time for daily or weekday meditations?
5. Are these times ever wasted?
6. Are breath exercises relevant?
7. Discuss a few disciplines concerning food, and list some foods to be avoided.
8. What admonitions are given concerning clothing?
9. What is the thrust of the message from ORPHIEL?
10. List some possible physical effects of cosmic contact.
11. Discuss color and its relation to communication.
12. What is the function of a symbol in telepathic communication? How are they used in conveying Truth?

NOTES

X
The Dynamics of Attunement

Proper attunement is absolutely vital to wholesome and productive cosmic telepathy. We will approach the process in five specific steps. As an aid to memory when you are sitting in a softly lit room or any location where following the print in a book would be awkward, I am suggesting that you let the fingers of your left hand be your memory guide. We will label each finger as a step in the process, and all you will need to do is memorize the step associated with each finger. Your mind will trigger the details of each step, so that wherever you may be, you can hastily touch each finger and breeze through the attunement process and make your contact.

The five steps are:
1. RELAXATION AND AFFIRMATION (Be still and know)
2. INVOKE THE LIGHT (Protection)
3. VISUALIZATION AND RESONANCE (Raising the energy level)
4. SPECIFIC CALL AND INVITATION (Requests, needs, questions)
5. OPEN THE RECEIVING CIRCUIT (Passivity)

1. Beginning with the thumb, touch your thumb with the other hand and say out loud, "Be still...and KNOW!" Being

123

still is known by many terms. It has been called entering the silence, or being in tune with the Infinite. Whatever you term it, it is a stillness that must permeate every level of being. Obviously it begins with the body. A quick way to accomplish this is to visualize yourself falling through space gently, and softly landing in the chair where you are, like a laundry softener commercial. Most all of us know of placing the hands palm upward in the gesture of receiving, letting the wrists fall casually across the thighs. But did you know that the soles of the feet are also prominent receivers? An array of small vessels there also helps in your receptivity, along with the hands. The open palms and the soles of the feet turned sideways can make a difference. A holy custom of long ago was to remove the shoes in a holy place. In your privacy, let the feet be bare, if possible. The sole of the foot is an intake area; doubtless this is why in yoga positions the soles are upturned.

Secondly, still the emotional body. Cleanse the heart of everything but peace and love. Cover everything else that would enter with a cloak of Love. Spend much time in this practice of total relaxation and emptying of the emotions and cares of everyday living. If extreme tenseness is present, then you may need to speak to each portion of the body, telling it to relax, beginning with the feet and coming all the way up to the scalp, literally telling each portion to relax; even the face muscles, and the tightness of the scalp covering, all of the many neck muscles. Let the mouth droop open if necessary, but somehow, some way, get yourself relaxed. Each moment spent in trying will make it easier and faster to accomplish the next time, until finally you will only have to give the body one command to relax and instantaneously it will be done. Achieve relaxation!

Then, coupled with final relaxation, very peacefully one gives some form of affirmation. If this is new to you, begin simply with the Lord's Prayer, a wonderful attunement vehicle. Or, at this quiet point, one could give the three breaths using the

OHM vibration. In some manner at this point, you are going to *remind yourself* of your inner divinity, your God image, your own indwelling Christ Presence. You may acknowledge "I Am That I Am" and repeat it until you know that you are.

You are also a being of Light, so affirm it by repeating, "I Am a Child of the Light. I serve with the Brotherhood of Light to bring Light upon this planet." Or use the magnetizing affirmation given by Ashtar in *Project: World Evacuation* on page 183, which affirms as follows:

"I AM...a Guardian of the Light!

"I AM...Love in Action here!

"Cooperating with the Ashtar Command.

"I AM dedicated to

"• The Kingdom of God on Earth

"• Interplanetary Fellowship

"• and Universal Peace"

Or simply affirm, "I AM a child of God embodied upon this planet to serve the will of my heavenly Father; so be it."

2. An affirmation is the act of positively asserting a fact which you KNOW to be truth! So in this moment of your stillness you affirm to yourself and all of heaven above that which you know, and you know that you know...and it strengthens the sense of your own spiritual authority to engage in the steps that follow. *KNOW WHO YOU ARE, WHERE YOU CAME FROM AND WHY YOU ARE HERE, AND DO NOT HESITATE TO SPEAK THE WORDS OF YOUR CHRIST PRESENCE.*

3. At this point in step one, there are thousands of New Age children of Light who are now turning to the assistance of quartz crystals in their attunement. This is a valid and worthwhile supplement to attunement which is now being encouraged by the higher realms for our day. Crystals are frozen solidified Light. Quartz crystal is a power source that comes from ALL THAT IS. Crystals beam back with intensity, the reverence which you invite. Beautiful, large, and colorful crys-

tals have found their way into my hands. I was taught by Hilarion how to use the crystal. I recommend it highly for use with meditation.

When in the process of attuning to receive cosmic telepathy, hold your crystal to your forehead just above and between the physical eyes, directly in front of the pituitary gland. A moderate, firm pressure here with the crystal throughout the attunement steps will increase the activity of this important gland. When desiring to send or transmit your message, hold the crystal on the top of the head above the crown chakra, directly above the pineal gland, just over the "third eye," for a higher degree of thought-force.

STEP NUMBER 2, SECOND FINGER: INVOKE THE LIGHT! Light is the most powerful emanation in all Creation. The need to employ LIGHT in any activity is imperative, and daily becoming more so. Employ the LIGHT in every area of your life. Do not use in a casual way...its power is inconceivable. It needs merely to be INVOKED! It knows what to do, where to go and how to function. When you INVOKE THE LIGHT, you are commanding that God's Will be done. You cannot abuse the Light; it does not have any negative quality, and we become more radiant by using it. Any form of dark emanation cannot face the LIGHT and will flee from it when IT IS INVOKED for that purpose. Negativity cannot stand in its presence and is dissolved when the LIGHT IS INVOKED into a situation. Mischievous, malignant, harmful spirits, incarnate or discarnate, cannot abide in the LIGHT. When it is INVOKED FOR THEIR REMOVAL, they vanish. Learn, PLEASE...TO INVOKE THE LIGHT!

As soon as your feet hit the floor in the morning, INVOKE THE LIGHT upon your whole being and your personal world. INVOKE THE LIGHT when you leave your home for the pathways of the world. But most of all, do not enter meditation, do not even consider it, until you have INVOKED THE LIGHT FOR YOUR PROTECTION! State that you will not receive the words of any being who does not serve the Golden White LIGHT of God, in heaven or on earth.

Then use that Light to build your form of protection. Some like to construct a great tube of LIGHT which reaches upward into infinity while they sit at its point, which touches earth. Others visualize a great milk bottle shaped cone of LIGHT in which they sit, while some construct a PYRAMID OF LIGHT. A great many meditators construct a circle of LIGHT around them, a ring pass-not of impenetrable protection. Personally, I prefer to construct a sphere of Light in which I position myself. It covers me above, beneath, to the right, to the left, before, and behind, and within my being. It is a veritable solid ball of pure Golden-White LIGHT, and I KNOW...as *you* must *know*, absolute protection. When you have adequately enfolded yourself in the Christ LIGHT—an armor of Divine Love—when you know you are sheltered and protected from negativity in any form, then and only then do you progress to Step 3. For anything that is unlike the LIGHT or is in disharmony with it, cannot remain within it.

• • •

STEP NUMBER 3, THIRD FINGER: VISUALIZATION AND RESONANCE are employed to raise your energy level. Now you take the impenetrable White Christ LIGHT and begin to work with it within your whole being, to flood yourself with it. As you are sitting totally relaxed, invoke the Golden LIGHT consciously, and direct it into the area of the brain. Flood it all through the cortex rim and command it to be still, subdued by God's LIGHT. Flood the LIGHT into that great idle portion, command the tensor sector to arise and awake to assist you to manifest the God Power that is already yours. Consciously direct the LIGHT down the spine, stopping at each chakra area to flood that chakra with Golden Light— the throat chakra, the heart chakra, down the spine to the solar plexus, then the lower chakras. Following this, consciously slowly pull the Golden LIGHT back up the spine, stopping once again to flood each chakra as you pass by. Your crystal may be employed here also, touching the area of the chakras as the Golden Light enfolds each one. Finally, return the stream of Golden Light back up to the top of the head and the crown chakra, taking all that you need, filling yourself with it; then release it to circle around the world. You are now a radiating, emanating, great beam of LIGHT.

6. Now to resonate your vortex...realize that every living cell within you is a receiving antenna. Start from the feet area and visualize a swirling stream of energy rotating around your feet. Build that swell of energy until it rises higher and higher; until this circular winding of white energy—in tornado-like fashion—flows around the legs, the thighs, whirling in atomic action all around you. This is your own resonating electromagnetic pulsation. See it whirling around your middle, your chest cavity, your shoulders, neck and head. Now you are a swirling vortex of golden LIGHT, a scintillating mass of nuclear energy.

Now, very slowly, let it unwind back down again to your feet. This has been a deliberate act of resonance, raising you and your crystal to a high level of divine energy and creating a strong vortex for communication. You have awakened the sleeping dynamics of your higher consciousness, without which, you are nothing. See yourself, then, in all of His Likeness, His stalwart son or daughter, capable of anything, equipped to master every challenge, to conquer every foe, to move undaunted into the fray, to dare, to do, and to accomplish what our world ignorantly calls "miracles." You are Master, if you choose to be. Now you are ready to give your call to higher planes *on your authority* as an embodied son or daughter of God, which compels the answer!

• • •

STEP NUMBER 4, FOURTH FINGER: SPECIFIC CALL AND INVITATION, which will also encompass your requests, needs and questions. To be specific, this is that point where you deliberately call for Spirit Cooperation. Remember that all things which come to you pass through or are permitted entrance into your human forcefield by your own Christ Presence, or Higher God-self.

8. Cosmic Teacher Aljanon has given us this call to be used: "I, as a son/daughter of the New Age awakening now upon the earth, command forth in the name of my Mighty I AM PRESENCE, that my Holy Christ Self flow forth into my human mind and perform the work of reuniting me to its God-Receiver. Come into me now, Oh Christed One, and raise me back up to my Source. Bring forth God energies necessary for me to know only the Perfection of God Love, Life and Light this day in all I see, speak, and do. So be it done in the name of My Mighty I AM PRESENCE." (He also explained that with each use of this call, new synaptical junctions will take place in nerve endings that have long remained dormant).

9. Now you are ready to continue the "Call": "In the Name of God I AM THAT I AM and in the Name of Jesus the Christ, I invoke the presence and help of heaven's invisible army, the Angels, the Light Bearers of the Universe, the Brotherhood of Light, our Space Friends of other worlds, the Avatars, the Masters, the Teachers, the Healers, and all of those who work within my own lifestream to guide, to teach, to protect; to receive the love I now send to them and to assist me in my endeavor to find and to manifest God's will for my life, now at this very moment. I also specifically call to _____." Here one could insert the name of any particular one who is sought and state your reason.

In calling a specific Being, it helps to attempt to visualize that one in their own setting or environment, as you also look upon a painting or picture of that one. Form a large tube or tunnel and picture the other person as appearing at the other end of it while you remain at this end. Formulate your thought or request with precision and definiteness. Attunement with this one will be recognized by a feeling of being connected mentally. As you awaken long dormant facilities, these procedures become smoother.

• • •

STEP NUMBER 5, LITTLE FINGER: OPEN THE RECEIVER CIRCUIT. This is the point of "active passivity." Remind yourself you are not going to fall asleep. As you still the mind, check the mental rush to create space. Spread out within that empty space the "outside yourself" feeling. Maintain strength to receive and spiritual alertness. Shut out the world and listen to the rhythm of your heartbeat, and relate it to the rhythm of the universe. Remember, telepathy is passive detection of a thought. Slow your thinking cortex down to a crawl, or ignore it completely. You are not concentrating on receiving; you are not thinking at all; you are passive, peaceful, receptive…but you *ARE LISTENING!* You are listening as the blind man listens to the television!

In my earlier sessions with my spiritual teachers, one was giving me a session on the art of listening. It was he who told me to listen as the blind man listens. He said he would produce several sounds which I was to identify. I identified the first one as the sound of snapping fingers; the second was the sound of slapping hands; the next sound reminded me of wind swishing by; then he said he would do One of the three, which I then identified. Then he gave me a sound which would be a spiritual symbol in the form of sound which would identify their presence to me. It was a "cool" lesson!

Students in the mystery schools of the Orient have 43 bells to identify. In another room, their teacher strikes one of the bells and the student can tell the teacher which bell is ringing because he has become attuned to the frequency of that bell.

For a considerable time I received a sound in one ear which I thought was physical. But when I sought an explanation, it was explained that the sound was not physical but one of the calling cards of my Heavenly Friends. It was similar to the sound of a loud cricket in the right ear. It proved to be an attention getter. I learned to enter another dimension when it was present, and a message would be waiting. This personal signal also was a precaution against any intrusion of unwelcome souls, being a personal signal between us.

So it is that we learn to listen to become aware. George Van Tassel has stated: "Thinking is the act of becoming aware of what already exists. One does not try to think to become aware. One only has to remove his own thoughts and then the Universal Mind rushes in to fill the void."

In the telepathic language, the medium is thought. Therefore, there is never a misunderstanding between communicants wherever in space they may be. The language of thought is not subject to semantic problems related to oral languages. One listens through thought.

While compiling this chapter, the I AM Presence overshadowed me with this poignant plea to be included. It seems to be addressing traditional Christianity primarily:

"Tradition has adopted an attitude concerning the devotional life that produces limitation in their growth. In the multitude of words and repetitions, though well meant and sincere, there is a tendency to overspeak but not to *listen*. They come to the secret closet to pour out their heart and when they are finished, they immediately depart from that place. I desire to stress to those who know My Name and know My Being, to bring to that place a heart that *listens*, a heart that pauses for a response. This could change the entire outlook concerning petition and a Heavenly Father Who not only hears, but answers prayer even while they yet speaketh.

"Christians, so-called, must learn to be still within themselves, to enter the silence of their devotional hour, to hold the soul motionless in its attention upon the Father and His responses. O do let the still small voice, so soft, so still within thee, speak its words to thee, and be quiet within thee, that it might be heard. O the moments of beauty and growth that are lost for want of a moment longer to linger in His Presence.

"Thy Father will not turn thee away unanswered, but will, with every cry of your heart, respond with a message of guidance and comfort from deep within thy heart. Be not noisy in approach to spiritual matters or too quick to leave the citadel of fellowship with Spirit.

"Christianity has forsaken true meditation upon the Voice of God. I plead with thee, My Loving Hearts, to forsake your petitions and let the Spirit of God fulfill every need that exists within your being and your life. For doth the Spirit not know every detail that pertains to thee and doth not Spirit also know just how to provide those needs and take care of thee? Then forsake thy demands and give thyself to periods of silence in His Presence, only to think, O Father, how lovely is Thy Work and how marvelous all Thy Ways and how magnificent it is to be in Thy Presence.

"For where the thought travels, the energies do follow. To think of the Celestial Kingdom and those who abide therein is to transport thyself to that place. Howbeit thine own heart is also the abode of the Highest of All. Commune with thine own heart. Let every beat of thy heart count as an age of time when He hath loved thee. So let it be that a moment of stillness with God will soften all the other moments of thy day and smooth out thy difficulties as if by miracle yet not miracle, but an attracting of emanations to thyself which thou art already sending forth. And thus your own environment will reflect around you the peace that abides within thyself.

"Then I would ask of those who are called by My Name and who would know my voice, sit thyself down and in quietness let thy soul become motionless, stilled in the innermost parts of being, that you might listen. Think not of anything or naught that troubles thee, but lay all aside and relax in the knowing of My Love for thee, that I care for thee and that I am ever with thee and will never leave thee.

"Rejoice that you are overshadowed by the Presence and that your moment of motionless passivity turned toward Me will fill you with rivers of peace. Thine ears shall hear a word and thy heart shall understand that word. This I call unto thee to do, and lay aside thy much speaking but rather, to learn to *listen* for the Voice of thy God.

"I AM THAT I AM hath spoken these words unto thee who will read and heed for thy self's sake."

Listening has always held a prominent part in a fruitful devotional life!

In conclusion, may I apologize for the many words used to probe the depths of these five steps of attunement—their details, their mechanics. But actually, they are not that involved or profound. In reality, the steps are simple. The Teachers request that the details of the five steps be read five times to absorb their Light, to understand the basic principles.

Then memorize the five finger steps. If you have to print on each finger with a pen the name of that step, by all means do it! But learn them, so that you can easily reconstruct them with your *eyes closed*. When you can do this, my mission is completed, and it becomes your responsibility from there.

Return to the first page of this chapter and, taking them finger by finger, once more, name the five steps in successful cosmic telepathy.

Think on These Things

1. How would you instruct a beginner in meditation to relax the body?
2. Explain the term "AFFIRMATION" and how it is used in the text.
3. Have an open discussion on the place of crystals in meditation.
4. Discuss LIGHT and tell why it must be invoked in spiritual activity.
5. What is the "LIGHT-VISUALIZATION" exercise?
6. What is meant by "resonating magnetic pulsation?
7. What is a vortex?
8. How do you call forth the Christ Self?
9. Discuss the components of the larger call to heaven.
10. Debate: Should one call a specific Being in certain cases?
11. How do you open the receiving circuit?
12. Can you name the five steps of attunement?

NOTES

XI
The Dynamics of Accuracy

An apostle of the Lord Jesus once said, "If any speak, let them speak as the oracles of God" (1 Peter 4:11). This, of course, is the goal of all, but the honest admit that no sensitive has absolutely perfect sensitivity at *all* times. In this chapter we will examine this phenomenon and attempt to find some of its causes to better improve ourselves.

The well-integrated are energized by their work, when undertaken within reason, but most cannot work from one to three hours without fatigue affecting accuracy. For the present, we will set aside the ever-present interference of the Dark Ones, but whenever this is suspected or evident, it must be resolutely and fearlessly dealt with.

1. Our attention is focused upon the activity of discernment as it applies to the messages received, to discern between a source of little understanding and the Cosmic Man. Thoughts projected from lesser beings will contain discriminations, divisions, judgments and personal feelings. The highly evolved Source will manifest love, understanding and compassion without being judgmental. A message should be for the purpose of uplifting the soul—certainly never for the intention to entertain or tell fortunes. The purpose should be to guide an individual into worthwhile thoughts which ultimately lead to worthwhile deeds. If enough souls become involved in worthwhile deeds, the world becomes a lighter, brighter and better place.

The beginning activities of Cosmic Telepathy will doubtless bring some confusion, but for those who persevere, this confusion will also finally disappear. We need to remember that the content of first messages is primarily to maintain interest. Rarely are they attempting to say anything profound, but rather, to stimulate reaction. While you are concerned with the content, your communicator is concerned with your process of achievement. However, if you reach a point of disgust and discouragement to the danger point of quitting, they will muster their force for complete accuracy, since the goal is development of high receptivity.

2. Certain factors in discernment have been given by great teachers in times past. For example, never approach communication from an emotional angle. Never approach to receive communication from the dead. Never become too involved in messages that are too visionary, that do not keep human or takes you off the job—quit cold. The interest of the one desiring communication should be for exploring truth, knowledge and understanding. There are a few examining pointers to consider in any material. Ask yourself whether it glorifies God; does it tend to uplift humanity? Does it have ideals that are constructive? Does it call forth respect from one who reads it? Primarily, contact is for betterment of human living and not for any psychic development. The first objective is perfecting your method of communication, followed by the second objective— to absorb the spiritual principles into the mental structures and expand the consciousness to understand that which is received.

3. We are here to learn discrimination; it is one of life's lessons. We do recognize and honor the Christ Presence in all men, but we also come to learn that *all living souls are at a different stage along the pathway of evolution.* Likewise, all heavenly communicants are themselves traversing the etheric realms at different levels of attainment. The goal of all communication should be to contact the highest realms possible, through the highest possible motivation. We must realize that all holy

agents will give forth on the level of their attainment and the revelatory output of their messengers will correspond to the level of their mentors. The Universal Law that states that "Like attracts like" comes into action here. Therefore, the more highly evolved the telepath, the higher and purer ill be the revelation. For the highly evolved raise themselves to upper levels, above astral forces. Master Jesus taught us to be fruit inspectors, and we may examine a telepathic message with just as much discernment as we would listen to a message from behind a pulpit. Avoid all messages that feed the human ego. A true Teacher will appeal to the highest and best in our nature and call forth our very soul. Learn discrimination!

As mentioned above, we are also here to learn discernment, another of life's lessons. Whenever doubt or question is present, GO WITHIN to your own Christ Self, your God Self, and seek guidance. Our Christ Presence is an infallible source of all Universal Light and Wisdom. If we were "spoon-fed" by the Higher Ones, we would never develop the discernment *so needed farther along the pathway.* Love impels the mother eagle to thrust the young from out of the nest. Truth is truth to us when we know it within ourselves. *Knowing* is an inner conviction projected by our own Christ Presence. If any embodied person attempted to change our knowing with an opposing assertion, inwardly we would sigh, immediately recognizing that person's location upon the pathway as "just not *there* yet." Likewise, we do the same with any disembodied soul. They, also, will be taught farther along the pathway. One who takes negation into transition will continue to cling to a false concept until his mind is opened to receive higher teachings. The fact of being discarnate *is not any sudden bestower of wisdom!* Wisdom from many other lives is stored in the causal body of the soul/mind, and how often it develops that the one who finds himself in the position of student is really the teacher, and the one in the position of teacher is really the student. Expect this occasionally, and learn discernment.

So often we need to tune out to tune in. We are surrounded by thought patterns of avarice, personal judgments and worries. An evolving messenger must constantly protect the mind against receiving these impressions. We must attempt to keep our thoughts on a level that will attract the emanations we desire. We must constantly recognize the character of these worldly impressions.

Discordant thought is harmful from wherever it is received. Often a message will contain gems of Higher Truth easily recognizable and because of their presence, an entire message will be accepted, though it may contain divisions and personal promises, and discriminations. We must learn to discern these things. Neither do our Space Brothers condemn us for our shortcomings; they know we are behaving according to our understanding. Whether we are in touch with a higher or a lower level, our own minds operate in the ruts of our own understanding. It is always wise to keep a journal in which the entries of your contacts can be made. These can be studied over a period of time for better clarity of a message that seems to permeate several.

• • •

4. Part of the important process of discernment is learning to "try the spirits whether they be of God" (1 John 1:4). Any communicant may be challenged to affirm whether or not he honors the Lord God of Hosts, or serves Jesus the Christ, or will acknowledge to Be within the Light of God. One may INVOKE THE LIGHT OF GOD, and if any are not of that Light, they cannot abide within it and will have to leave.

Telepathy is an impersonal universal principle. As you are, so will you attract. It behooves us to live the most spiritual life possible. It literally means walking in all of the Light that you have attained. It is living your Light that makes it your own and a part of you, impregnated into all levels of your being. It means conquering every challenge that your Light has given you, so that you can be readied for more knowledge and advancement. One cannot be slothful in spiritual attainments and expect to receive back through the superconscious mind, contacts from the highest and worthiest levels. Spiritual attainment is totally related to the nature of the telepathic communications that will feed back.

I once asked my Teachers to discuss false messages from the astral levels, and this was the reply:

"When one strays from the pure stream, one must expect to find streams of polluted waters if one is unfamiliar with the terrain. All spirit has vision superior to the earthly mortal, but all have not learned how to present or evaluate their envisioned facts. There is such an eagerness present to respond that care is not weighed in the responsiveness. Much too often they are filled with an anxiety to create some emotional reaction, especially those of lower plane development; hence, a tendency to dogmatic statements and derogatory platitudes. If the statement appears to be emphatically sure, then it probably is not."

I have learned also, that verbosity is not necessarily the criterion of eternal verities. Some telepathic comments may be too heavenly and flowery to be of any earthly use. Master Jesus sounded the keynote in the simplicity of his methods. As for me, I try hard to fulfill the admonition above my desk: "Keep it simple, stupid!"

4. Luciferian brothers are probably best known for their attributes as deceivers and plainly they are liars. Commander Anton reinforces the concept of checking out all would-be communicators: "It is a very wise procedure to diligently require identification information and the relationship of the speaker to the Divine Program of Light in heaven and on earth. The Lord's Hosts to not ever mind taking the time to acknowledge their Light. Demand to know the spiritual standing, and it will be freely given. Those who thus refuse or evade are to be avoided as imposters and will not remain in the Light which is held up to them. They will withdraw when properly

challenged. This examining of identity and spiritual status must not be taken lightly nor overlooked. However, those of the highest vibrations of love and understanding will immediately perceive a lesser vibration as it enters their awareness in communication."

"The seed atom of Light within those who serve the Light is always instantly recognized by those who manifest it. We who serve the Light Universally and upon the planet are all a part of the Lord's Hosts and serve under the banner of our Beloved Commander, Jesus the Christ and Lord of this Galaxy. We welcome the challenge and honor any who takes the time to ask of us. We would seriously warn all who enter this pursuit, that your own motivations must be of the purest nature and for the purpose of expanding the Light upon your planet. This warning is important, for you will attract to your own force-field that which is most like you in thought, word, and deed. I am Anton."

• • •

We move along now to another factor, probably the most prominent of all in creating error or illusion in Cosmic Telepathy, and that is the destructiveness of emotional or mental involvement in that which is coming through. Our own thinking and human feeling is the greatest barrier to smooth communication. If we dissect or examine every statement as it comes through, then we are not passive and therefore, not proceeding properly, and our own thoughts will be that which is recorded. We absolutely MUST withdraw the human personality from any phase of spiritual work.

I have a very fine message from Beloved Athena which came in response to my question, "What is the lesson of illusion?"

Athena responded: "Illusion is an aura of error self-created, and accepted as it appears. The (self) deceived soul is enmeshed in a web of erroneous thought which has been created by the subconscious mind. This is a common trap for beginners with spiritual awareness. The mind has not learned to *STEP ASIDE*, and therefore, involves itself in the messages that are received.

"Strictest discipline is required to acquire perfect concentration and purity of contact. The Masters do not send forth error, but truth is often distorted and clouded by the messenger. Whenever there is the slightest inclination to *race ahead in thought or to respond to that which is being transmitted, CLOUDING MAY RESULT.* Human reaction and human response must be laid aside, as well as maintaining *desirelessness* regarding the subject under discussion.

"The words come clear to the dedicated initiate and clouding is only present whenever self-desire or feelings intrude into the communication. Never assume that you know what is being said or about to be said, or that wisdom is present regarding the subject! Let the comment be completed without passing any human judgment.

"Human excitement triggers the imagination into construction of details that are not always present in the original transmission. When one is attempting to receive a message for one's personal self, unless one is very disciplined in concentration, the emotions become involved in the transmission as well as its solutions. Human desire can color the message, and the ray aspect will color its phrasing. These must be recognized and ruthlessly sifted out. With proper control, any channel should be able to receive a message for themselves just as clearly as they receive any other message. It is not factually true that one cannot receive for themselves dependably, when sufficient training has been undertaken. Remember at all times to keep oneself separated from the transmission that is received, with no emotional response to it, nor even any enthusiasm, because it only flows through you. It can be read later for discernment purposes. The Masters are often under great difficulty when their words—which are truth—must be subjected to human coloring.

"A messenger must think of himself as a telephone, through which a message is passed to another...inanimate, impartial, personal. It is much preferred to wait for a word to be repeated rather than racing off with it to some yonder conclusion. Learn to depend on one's sources. I am Athena who speaks."

Bad vibrations from another person in the environment of the communication can inhibit successful results, or the presence of one who is indulging in negative emotions. Further, we must learn to be happy. Do everything with joy. No task is irksome unless we give it the power to irritate us. We must work on our attitudes, for it is in the routine of living that our thought habits are formed. When one is happy, the mind cannot retain thoughts of anger, fear, anxiety or any destructive emotion. The Universal Law of Harmony relaxes the mind, releases tension in the body, and leads to successful telepathy. *A spiritual messenger must love and be loved to have free-flowing communication.*

• • •

The second culprit in destroying accuracy in communication is tension in the environment, stress, or illness! The better the health, the easier the contact. The better the nervous and spiritual control, the less likely a runaway into irrelevancies. The state of health definitely affects sensitivity, and even fluorescent lighting can disturb a sensitive. Incidentally, a spiritual sensitive requires only small doses of medication for the same results, as opposed to an unbalanced person or a mental patient, who require double or triple doses above the average person.

6. Often tension is present simply from overwork and the need of a good rest. Ashtar has a nice message concerning this: "The pacing of time in the life of a disciple is important in accomplishing all that must be done for the Light in the shortness of time that remains. Multitudes of voices call and lure the

inspired one away from their best avenue of expression. Pleasure and pursuits of a secular nature are ever present to detour the dedicated Light worker from the task. But those who have traveled far along the Pathway have come to recognize all such interference and are not thus distracted.

"However, I do stress the necessity of a time of coming apart to rest awhile, as taught by the Beloved, as very necessary. The great masters of the delicate concert instruments lovingly release the strings of their treasured instruments and allow them a time of loosening the tautness and the tightness and give them a rest, that their instrument will be all the more prepared to serve when the next appointment comes. There must likewise be space in the life of the most ardent devotee for relaxation of the pressures and the pull of great responsibilities. There must be a time of infilling the divine energies. Do not deny yourselves moments of withdrawal into peace, for when you return, the battle will still be there to be fought and won." I have appreciated those words, and I am also reminded that without the "rests" music would lose much of its beauty!

7. Anything that disturbs our peace disturbs our work as messengers. Emotional stress is not only a real killer, as science has learned, but it is total defeat to cosmic telepathy. One who is knotted within due to stress from environment cannot settle into the deep peace required for communication. Again, Ashtar has some well-chosen words on the subject of stress: "In times of emotional stress, it is helpful to pause and take a deep, long, slow breath. It is always beneficial to breathe deeply and slowly, at any time and under any circumstances. But in a time of emotional stress, one cuts himself off from spiritual help just when it is needed most. The glands become tense, and cannot feed into the four lower bodies as they would normally, when the body is suffering from emotional stress.

"Let this be the lesson—that emotional stress can be very detrimental to the process of receiving spiritual help to alleviate the *cause* of emotional stress. This is a fundamental lesson in mastery that I am sharing with you. We understand the pressures that come to all in the experience of embodiment. They are not easily endured. They can be destructive to the psyche and defeating to spiritual victory. Three long, deep breaths will always bring relief from pressures created by emotional tension or emotional responses to situations. As soon as circumstances permit, go within."

● ● ●

Many years ago the Arcana Workshops circulated a letter-article by Marguerite Rompage dealing with self-deception. It deals with persons who are rather emotional and impulsive by nature, unable to differentiate between their own inner wish life and their outer field of vision. She writes that as a person becomes preoccupied with heavenly contact as a possibility for themselves, the inner thought life and wish-life light up and become very important. To the self-centered, such preoccupation can become high intoxicating. It can transform the life of lonely people into constant adventure. Hypersensitive people who feel misunderstood or victims of unfriendliness find such preoccupation flattering and as a retreat from the demands and uncomfortable adjustments or normal human relations. Those who are timid and inexperienced in social contact, although spiritually awakened, enjoy spiritual communication because they don't have to meet others personally or engage in telephone conversations. Those who long only for psychic experience and desire an aura of mystery around their inner world find talking with invisible beings is just IT.

Mrs. Rompage readily admits that the above represents a stage through which everyone passes quickly on the way to full knowing—a stage which presents few demands and great satisfaction. She continues, "It is therefore not surprising to find many people lingering at this stage of experience, with no desire to move on! It is an irresponsible stage, so it is thoroughly enjoyed by the spiritual adolescent, who wants the utmost in colorful, novel experience but who is not mature enough to be held responsible for his speech, his temper, his behavior and his effect upon others."

In an effort to assist in distinguishing the true messenger from the false, she explains that a true Teacher will cause you to stand taller in the light of your own soul; will cause others to reveal and express the God within; and the Teacher will be a way into the community of souls, the Inner Community. There will be no self references to that extent, but the ideas used and expressed will appeal irresistibly to every soul who hears them. "You will look with the eye of the soul, listen with the ear of the soul, and will move in their direction." The letter was called "A Common Sense View," and it was certainly well named.

• • •

The third culprit who would destroy our accuracy and defeat our entire purpose...is...pride! Pride parades as unteachableness, self-exaltation, and arrogance. Sometimes the ego trip will deny progress to others to maintain their dependency. It expresses as, "My powers say to me...", etc. Pride is comfortable where it is and doesn't want to move on. The ego approach will eventually destroy all influence, and the lonely subject will wonder where it has all gone. The mechanical reaction of ego to all things asks "How will this affect ME?" Immaturity indulges in attention-getting statements, must dominate every conversation, and always tells all it knows to keep pace. Sheer force of verbosity may be its only ace in the hole! When I was a struggling student, my Teachers advised me, "Listen to the quiet man who speaks seldom; he will have something to say."

The material received by Robert Renaud from his Space contacts has a very pointed reference to these spiritual failures, which is quoted here:

"Those who merely are in the movement for profit, for

egoistic reasons, for publicity, or for the sake of perpetrating a hoax, will shortly find themselves dropped from the roster. They will be left behind in the coming insurgence of the movement. They are the ones who, in a very few years, will become the forgotten ones.

"On the other hand, those who find it in them to truly live as they have learned, and who are willing to work for others as well as for themselves, will find themselves to be integral parts of a growing, dynamic movement, soon to be a major factor in world affairs.

"We of other planets frankly admit that some of our choices were blunders, and we're willing to prove that we have learned by our mistakes. We are going to make up for lost time, my friends. There has been too much delay because of these unwise choices.

"Therefore, if they choose to remain as they are now, we will turn to new avenues of activity. There are many who would be very good for our purposes, and we will turn our attention from the old, outdated and now useless ones to fresh, new, and dedicated individuals.

"We have a grand message to deliver to you, the people of Earth. We are annoyed that it has been lost because of the ways of those to whom we have given the responsibility for this message."

• • •

This, then, leads us to the concept of accountability. At this point, I am privileged to quote a beautiful passage from Cosmic Master Lytton in 1982, through spiritual messenger LYARA—words filled with insight, depth and finality:

"Truth is not to be confused with illusions or delusions. Truth is the reality of living, moving, and being in harmony with the God Self at any given moment in time or experience. It requires the personal integrity to reach down deep enough to observe the soul as total calm or with ripples. The calmness is the center, the *knowing*.

"Within the evolution of mankind, man's greatest challenge has been to *know and conquer his emotions* to arrive clearly and purely at that center. From the center you understand that all ideals, belief systems, and concepts are Truth at *some level of reality*—of 'soul unfoldment' on our journey fully and completely back to the Source.

"Since ALL is God, no judgment need be rendered. What is judgment and how does it differ from discernment? Judgement is discerning a situation with emotional attachment. Discernment is the Science of Wisdom, of knowing. From the center of Peace, you will understand the laws of the Universe and how they are interpreted and processed by Life.

"God is Wisdom, and the more you unfold unto the depths of His Being, the more you will know that all is Love."

10. Love in Cosmic telepathy will always be geared toward growth. It will advance the individual beyond the original point of attraction. It will relate what you are doing to the whole. It will take no thanks to itself, knowing it is a transmitter only. It will deliver the intent of the message. It knows that even with a negative message, it has a choice in the manner of delivery. Love, seeing an umbrella symbol, might say, "You are beautifully protected," while another might say, "You're going into a terrible storm!" Love will not dramatize or jar the other person; no positive force transmits negative information. A ladder is a ladder and its steps are all part of that ladder—highest good or lower good.

Love knows that everyone must learn to function for themselves. Love will not create dependency on itself or tie anyone to itself. All of life is a series of opportunities for making decisions. These decisions form or destroy character. Love knows that making decisions for another deprives that one unwarrantedly of an opportunity for character growth. A loving and wise telepath will never make decisions for another. We cannot attend the school of life for another. We can offer a helping hand or a guiding word, but at no time may we force our will upon another. That one may be struggling to learn the lessons we have already mastered, so that he must master them himself.

Courtesy is Godly on any dimension. I had an acquaintance once—a gifted telepath—whose habit it was to interrupt any group or private conversation by suddenly placing her hand on her forehead and signaling everyone else to shut up, so to speak, because "something was coming through!"...doubtless of world-shaking significance, one was left to think. After a few evenings exposed to this individual, Teacher Herodotus spent one entire period setting me straight on "The Art of Poise While Receiving." Apparently my good friend had "had it," and he forcefully began:

11. "Undignified delivery colors content. DO NOT BE RUDE! Do not ever interrupt the conversation of another to flaunt *my* words. Courtesy is an attribute of the universe, and no higher being may carelessly set aside its law without loss of respect for his high calling. The words of one of any dimension whatever, must await his turn to be heard, the same as the incarnate. Courtesy is the mark of the saint; rudeness, the hallmark of the untrained." Strangely enough, at my next private visit with the lady, her Guidance came and apologized for his rudeness. So Herodotus must have been a little busy in the interim!

12. Just one more thought concerning accountability, and we will move along. Unfortunately, there are those few whose ego has convinced them that because they have decided to follow the disciple's path and save the world, they are justified in totally deserting their little children, their spouse, their jobs, and that any and every commitment or vow entered into may casually be tossed aside. While a true World Server will not refuse to do the work of the Light, neither will he leave unfinished any part of his life's pattern. He will avoid all future karma by working out all relationships involved until there is

total Peace within himself, and all of the emotional ties and obligations of the Great Law are satisfied. The "fabric of life" will be handled so that freedom prevails for all that are concerned. This right attitude will automatically bring heavenly assistance into any situation, however complicated it may be. We may not leave our personal responsibilities to another without the retribution of a future encounter with that selfsame situation once again. Action and reaction applies even to the most ardent disciple.

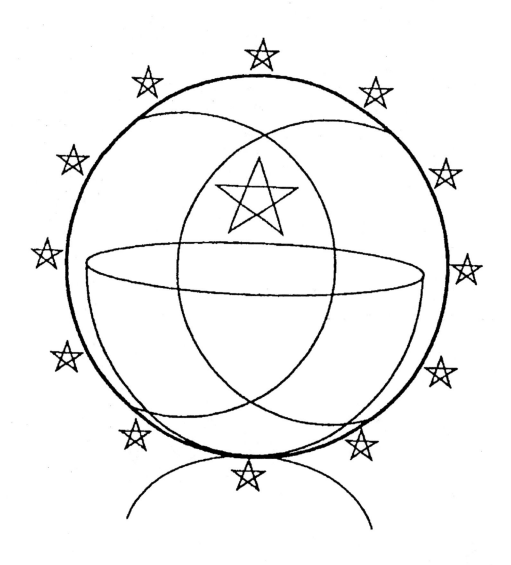

Think on These Things

1. How do you discern the level of a telepathic message?
2. Give some rules relating to the approach to communication.
3. What is the "level" of all spirit communication?
4. How do you "challenge" a spiritual Being?
5. Discuss Athena's explanation of illusion and error: what it is, how it is created, and what is its result (this portion of this chapter must be *thoroughly studied* and discussed).
6. What does Ashtar say about tension?
7. How does emotional stress affect telepathy?
8. Describe emotional immaturity and its reasons for seeking cosmic communications.
9. Discuss and identify the acts of pride and its fruits.
10. Explain the action of love in messengership.
11. How is courtesy applied to messengership?
12. How does the Law of Karma apply to a spiritual messenger?

NOTES

XII
The Dynamics of Service

Each man comes into the earth realm with a personally cho-sen purpose. The purpose was determined by his Spirit Soul at the hour of personal judgment in the halls of death (this being that place where newly arrived souls go for their evaluations).

The trend of the earth life will continually attempt to pull the physical circumstances toward that purpose, and if the soul is of a flexible and pliable nature, it will eventually find itself standing upon the threshold of its divine purpose. This may be recognized as such, or it may not, depending upon develop-ment and sensitivity.

1. Psychiatry calls these things "drives"; we prefer to think of them in terms of a spiritual undertow which pulls the earth life in a certain direction. Along with this pull, there may or may not be an accompanying array of talents which would make that way seem easier or more feasible. Universal Forces work together to help Soul find its fulfillment. For if destiny is thwarted, the incarnation has been a loss. Ah, this is the sor-row. So many fall away and become ensnared, so that the still, small voice within cannot be heard because of the nature of earth life.

The spiritually aware person will cooperate with the Over-soul in its strivings. We can know when self within is striving with us. Religiously speaking, we may call it "checks of the spirit"; medically speaking, we may call it guilts or complexes;

socially speaking, we may call it frustrations and providences, but all in all the sum total is, that Soul within is making itself heard through the din of mundane affairs.

When a man feels a strong spiritual undertow of conscience, or duty, or ideals, he should respond to these positive emotions, for these are the voice of the Oversoul, and if he denies them utterance his goal may be lost. Yes, goal...not *soul.* (It is impossible to lose your soul, for you ARE your soul). However, we may cause the soul to suffer unspeakable regret in the judgment time and immeasurable delay in its progress, by placing stumbling blocks in its path through dominant negative will. *WE SHOULD GIVE OURSELVES THE BENEFIT OF THE DOUBTS THAT BESET US,* for we are better than we think and we are more capable than we think; we have undreamed of hidden talents, abilities and strengths within us. We have access to vast storehouses of experiences, stored by us in *other lifetimes,* which are freely ours to draw upon for this life's decisions.

Life's highest plan is God's Will.

In Philippians 3:13 the apostle of the Lord wrote: "...this one thing I do, forgetting those things which are *behind,* and *reaching* forth unto those things which are before...." This epistle was written by Paul during his imprisonment in Rome. Surely if anyone would be justified with an attitude of satisfaction and complacency, he would be. "Behind" was the memory of his glorious conversion; "behind" were those three great missionary tours where thousands had been literally swept into new Light; "behind" was the launching of the Great Commission; "behind" were "labors abundant, stripes above measure, prisons, rods, stones, journeys and perils," but that great soul was not tempted to rest on past laurels and accomplishments. Dear One, the best that has happened to you thus far on the pathway should not be the yardstick for the rest of your life. There must still be a reaching forth to things yet greater to come. For beyond our best there are yet breadths, and lengths, and depths, and heights, and things that are yet undreamed of in our conception of the Grace and Power of Our Father in His Love for us! For all of us, there is a great *need* to go on!

2. Perhaps you have heard about the little fellow who fell out of bed in the night, telling his mommy, "I fell asleep too near where I got in!" For one on the pathway of Spiritual Awakening, that is also a dangerous place to fall asleep. The apostle had said, "...*reaching*". The dictionary has it as "stretching out..." as a limb, suggesting to us a living, growing thing; to "seize," "come to," "arrive at," "attain," "to grasp, to *strain after something.*" One of our poets has said it in this manner: "A man's reach should exceed his grasp, *or what's a heaven for?*" What indeed! In the 42nd Psalm, the writer cried, "As the hart panteth after the water brooks, so panteth my soul after thee, O God!" Beloved, do you pant after God like that? Again, the psalmist says, "With my soul have I desired thee in the night. I stretch forth my hands unto thee, my soul thirsteth after thee." Dear friend, have you ever hungered and thirsted for God's will in your life like that? If you have, that hunger will be satisfied, and that thirst will be quenched with rivers of Living Water. Someone has said, "We take according to our size." If we are satisfied with our present experience, we have cut off all possibility of growth and fresh new experience.

3. This thirsting, this hungering, this flowing desire power, is the *secret* of going on! To quit "reaching" is to stagnate. It is written, "They go from *strength to strength*, every one of them...appeareth before God" (Ps 84:7), and "...he that hath clean hands shall be stronger and stronger" (Job 17:9). "...the path of the just...shineth *more and more*...." (Prov 4:18). "Beholding the Glory...we are changed...from glory to glory." That is the pull of the oversoul in spiritual progress; strength to strength, stronger to stronger, more and more, glory to glory. Fresh emergencies bring fresh power. Let nothing stop you from finding life's highest purpose—the Glory of God! The *secret* of going on is "pressing toward the mark" in

the certainty that guidance is present and "the stars are still there." We cannot live in the lowlands. God's call to service is definite, personal and authoritative, but it carries with it an irrevocable assurance that the Caller will assist the one that is called. Amos Wells has written some beautiful words, inspired by the consecration of Paul to answer the call that came to him:

"Whither, O Christ?" The vision did not say;
Nor did Paul ask, but started on the way.
If Paul had asked, and the Lord had said;
If Paul had known the long, hard road ahead;
If with the heavenly vision Paul had seen
Stark poverty with cold and hungry mien,
Black fetid prisons with their chains and stock,
Fierce robbers lurking amid tumbled rocks,
The raging of the mob, the crashing stones,
The aching eyes, hot fever in the bones,
Perils of mountain passes wild and steep,
Perils of tempests in the angry deep,
The drag of loneliness, the curse of lies,
Mad bigotry's suspicious, peering eyes,
The bitter foe, the weakly blundering friend,
The whirling sword of Caesar at the end—
Would Paul have turned back...with a shuddering moan
And settled down at Tarsus...had he known?
NO! and a thousand times the thundering no!
Where Jesus went, there Paul rejoiced to go.
Prisons were palaces where Jesus stayed;
With Jesus near, he asked no other aid;
The love of God kept him glad and warm,
Bold before kings and safe in the storm.
Whither, O Christ? The vision did not say.
Paul did not care, just started on the way.

● ● ●

We have come into the world as Lights. The Kingdom of

God is built by Light, clarifying Truth and expanding Understanding. We are here to radiate Light, to think Light, to use Light and to attract more Light to ourselves which we need to live as a creature of Light.

We are indebted to the Mark Age magazine under "Linking of Lights" for these very beautiful words:

4. "The most important work Light workers can do is to be the Light wherever they might be and project the Light into any condition of darkness and confusion. They must project the Light into the four corners of the world. In so doing, they are exacting a measure of Light enfoldment which will enable the Hierarchal Board to cleanse many conditions.

"Light workers have to live with the negation of mass consciousness, but they are also obliged to do everything they can to balance, to harmonize, and make possible for the mass mind to do exactly the work they have come to do. The Spiritual Hierarchy counts on all Bearers of the Light to hold the Light, be the Light, express the Light, and project the Light that the mass development upon this planet may be raised in consciousness. There is no other course in getting this planet straightened out and ready for its next dimensional expression and its role in the federation of planets within this solar system."

I was also impressed with these words of beloved Ashtar through another whose identity I do not know. He speaks:

"Live each day as if it were your last. Collect all of your mental baggage so that all which is of a lasting nature can be moved at once, all else left behind. Live so at any time or place you can turn your back upon the past without regret or backward glance. Gather unto yourself all your dreams and desires of service to God and man, for these are your wealth."

We are Sons and Daughters of God. We are all a part of the same part and are one. What He is, so are we, and the inner core of us is at One with Him. We agree in One with Him, in our hope, our purpose, our will. For we are all One Mind with the Father.

5. Yet we are individual also, with individual patterns cut upon our soul by virtue of our individual acts of individual lives. We have motivations and drives and various reactions to various circumstances that have all blended together to make us what we are. We are the sum total of all we have ever been. Nevertheless, within the inner core of Being, we are spirit-Gods also, with the full capacity of becoming that which we already are. If this were not true, we could not have communion and fellowship with the Father and His children. This inner core of spirit Being rises up and grabs something which we suddenly react to, with an inner knowing that it is Truth! It isn't recognition. It is more properly, *memory in action*. Awakening is in actuality a stirring of an old *memory*, like a sleeping animal hearing the sound of a familiar horn, or call. We remember because the inner core *always knew!*

6. It follows that the work of our lives (however many there have been) is the business of stripping the veneer of earth life thinner and thinner from *around* that inner core, so that it is released into contact with the Universal companionship that it requires. The outer layers of density absorbed from earth life must be penetrated like circumventing the doorman at an elegant occasion. Once the Heralds of Heaven can get past the doorman of our thinking brain and our reasoning, they can get through to our responsive soul and accomplish their work. The innermost self is the *real* you, which always was and always will be. The makings of a successful spiritual worker will be in proportion to their success in stripping down to that inner core of contact. For it is there that heaven speaks to us, reaches us, and impresses us. It is not clearly explainable, but the soul of you doesn't have any trouble at all hearing the heavenly speakers, understanding them, or accepting them.

• • •

My beloved friends, there is a *glory* in going on! Life's highest service is God's work. Paul's reason for forgetting things behind and reaching forth to the before, and for pressing toward the mark, was for "the prize of the high calling of God!" The same desire, the same spirit that caused you to first step upon the Pathway, should be an ever-increasing spiritual expansion and a continuing experience extending throughout your life.

I treasure these words that Ashtar sends to you:

"All of you are strategically placed to shine with confidence and faith as a Light to those who lack a deeper dimension of awareness. Therefore, now is the time to be strong in your witness of our presence, and the faithfulness of Our Radiant One.

"It is the demand of the times that proofs and material evidences be given, but no greater proof hath any man than the shining aura of faith and Light with the detailed guidance upon the pathway, of those who abide in the shadow of God! Let those who demand the physical things mock as they will, our beloved brothers and sisters upon the earth shine as great beacons in the darkness, and their presence has long held off many disasters said to come, but our diodes of Light remain therein.

"Follow your own inner awareness. Seek the message within thy Being. Know thyself and the splendor within and no harm shall befall thee. A Great Light has come upon the planet and a Great Influence toward that Light accompanies it. Sense this Light and feel its influence in all of your ministries and service.

"Now is the time when the stars shall sing for joy, but the darkness will comprehend it not. Awaken the Angel that is within thee and reach for the inheritance that is already thy very own. Radiant sons and daughters of the Most High, hold fast to all that has been told thee, and go in Peace. I am Ashtar."

A spiritual messenger friend from the Houston area sends along to us this contribution from the "Angels of the Yellow Ray of Wisdom" to share with you:

7. "When the Masters of God's Light, Love and Life look upon the earth in their searching for specific chelas to use as channels, they are interested in a few things. First, how clear is the channel. Second, what type of people will this information be allowed to reach. And thirdly, will the information be given out to as many of God's children as is humanly possible.

8. "Children, it is time to come together in common pools for the receiving, processing, and disseminating God's information throughout the earth. Put away the egos if they still walk with you. For the Father says, 'Walk upon this earth as I made you, child, and let My Love and My Wisdom and My Power lead you through life. As I AM, so you will do what your God has shown you is His Way.'

"We ask that all of you workers in God's service come together in His Oneness and Love and share what He has given forth. Put away the bickering about which path is best and know that *where each of you stand is best for you now.* Otherwise you would not be there. You have all earned the privilege to be where you are by previous use of God's energies. Now is the time to come under the big roof of God and by doing so, you will be of greater service to your brothers. We do not ask you to compromise your duties and beliefs in your individual paths, only to share what you have been given in hopes that in your unity, We, the Guides and Guardians of this earth may better be able to use you in our service to the planet. Unity has always been the Way of the Father. So be up now in the Name of the Universal Christ, as has been commanded of us, His servants."

Guardian Action is deeply moved by this appeal, and it has long been a dream and a desire to do this very thing—to pool the messages from everywhere, in an update bulletin of what the Voice of God is saying throughout the land. However, as yet it is but a dream, a desire. But be that as it may, those groups or individuals who participate in the ministry of this volume are invited to send along from time to time copies of what you consider to be your most important cosmic communications for certain periods. In combining the messages, one can discern a strong trend as well as confirmation in detail. These should be current receptions—clear, concise and factual. Not verbose pastoral generalities, but clean-cut facts from reputable sources and the best spiritual messengers in America. Perhaps together we can join forces and follow the admonition of the Angels of the Yellow Ray to "come together in common pools for disseminating God's information." Full credit and recognition will be given for all messages thus shared with the world concerning end time events, activities of the Confederation and its noble members, and up to the minute fiats of our Tribunals and guidelines on international affairs and current events. All of us combined ARE the Guardian Action of this planet; we are the watchmen on the walls!

• • •

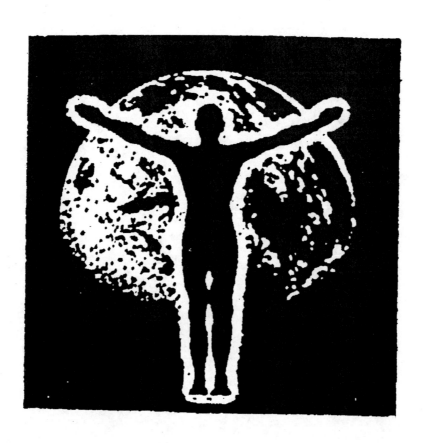

Think on These Things

1. What is meant by the pull of the Oversoul?
2. Define the word "reaching." How does it apply to spiritual activity?
3. What is the secret of "going on"?
4. What is the Light Worker's most important work?
5. Discuss the basis of our unique individuality.
6. How does the veneer of earth life hinder spiritual progress?
7. What do the Masters look for when searching for specific chelas?
8. Describe the plea of the Angels of the Yellow Ray and discuss your opinion of it.

NOTES

INNER LIGHT PUBLICATIONS PRESENTS
A TRIBUTE TO TUELLA

PRIMARY CHANNEL FOR THE ASHTAR COMMAND

Though she has passed from the physical realm, the channel Tuella remains the primary source of messages transmitted from the *Ashtar Command* , a spiritually advanced group of ETS who guide and instruct from a huge mother-ship circulation the earth at the equator. Before her transition to heavenly realms Inner Light purchased the rights to her monumental works and have endeavored to make them available to the public. The following titles are available directly from the publisher.

◆ *Ashtar: Revealing the Secret Identity of the*
Forces of Light and Their Spiritual Program For Earth

Here are messages from Ashtar, spokesperson for the Solar Council whose mission is to assist in our growth as planetary individuals and to offer warnings and advice in these monumental times. A delightful read for advancing souls! - $15.00

◆ *Project World Evacuation   (9th Printing)*

Will we be lifted off the planet in times of global disaster by friendly space beings lead by members of the Ashtar Command. Is this the rapture spoke of in the Bible? Where will the rescued be taken. What are we expected to bring with us during the exodus? - $21.95

◆ *A New Book Of Revelations*

Exposes the true meaning of 666. The special significance of the 13th Vortex. Corrects many inaccurate translations made of the Old and New Testaments and lays the foundation for a New World. - $16.00

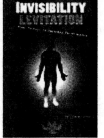
CONTINUED ON NEXT PAGE >